MEETING PEOPLE

A Hi-Lo Level 3-4 Story Collection for Adults

Sally J. Walker

Copyright 2019 Sally J. Walker
All rights reserved.

Printed in the United States of America

Published by Author Academy Elite
P.O. Box 43, Powell, OH 43035

www.AuthorAcademyElite.com

All rights reserved. No parts of this publication can be reproduced, stored in a retrieval system, or transmitted in any form or by any means—for example, electronic, photocopy, recording—without prior writer permission of the publisher. The only exception is brief quotations in printed reviews.

Paperback ISBN # 978-1-64085-938-8

Hardback ISBN # 978-1-64085-809-1

eBook ISBN# 978-1-64085-810-7

Library of Congress Control Number 2019910905

TABLE OF CONTENTS

Dedication v

Preface. vii

Yule Dogs of England, 1810 (An Historical) 1
1,941 words/4.3
    Glossary 9
    Mentor Questions. 11
    Possible Answers 13

A Hard Way to Go (A Western) 15
3,010 words/4.0
    Glossary 27
    Mentor Questions. 30
    Possible Answers 31

Dumb Animals Don't Think (A Western) 33
4,646 words/4.8
    Glossary 52
    Mentor Questions. 56
    Possible Answers 57

Tory Running (A Mystery) 59
6,136 words/3.8
    Glossary 83
    Mentor Questions. 86
    Possible Answers 87

The Gardner (A Romance) 90
3,361 words/3.5
    Glossary 104
    Mentor Questions...............................107
    Possible Answers 109

Roses for Annie (A Romance) 111
2,129 words/3.5
    Glossary 120
    Mentor Questions...............................122
    Possible Answers 123

Santa's Helper, or Not (A Romance) 125
4,152 Words/3.7
    Glossary 141
    Mentor Questions...............................145
    Possible Answers 147

DEDICATION

I want to dedicate this collection to the hungry readers of the world. When adults decide to learn how to read, they deserve to have fiction written at their level. Any fiction is meant to open minds to words, make-believe people, and fun.

PREFACE

Adult literacy will remain a problem in our world for many reasons, such as language barriers, poverty's lack of access to education and reading materials, and learning disabilities. Every human deserves to learn to read, not just to function, stay informed, and think in the 21st century's complicated world, but to discover how words, images, and make-believe can open the mind to possibility. Hopefully, this fiction work will motivate the hungry readers to search out more. Fiction for illiterate adults is not a waste of time, but a necessity. They deserve the opportunity to discover the fun of escaping into the imagination.

Each of these stories is presented with a glossary of words that may be unfamiliar to the reader and a list of comprehension questions and possible answers to assist the mentors guiding the reading of the illiterate adult. Professional educators working in the reading field have edited the stories, glossaries, and questions to assure mentors and readers that the stories contain adult content at Levels 3 and 4 reading ability. I thank reading specialist/educator Dr. Jean Lukesh for her careful, invaluable assessment of the stories and her contribution to the glossaries, story questions, and answers. Her examples and suggestions guided my revisions.

The historical is a story of English traditions and the meaning of giving.

The westerns present characters experiencing life west of the Mississippi in the late 1800's. The reader will discover the risks and joys of frontier challenges lived in a rugged environment.

MEETING PEOPLE

The mystery is a contemporary story about a young woman coping with loss and an eerie spirit trying to get the attention of a protector.

The romantic stories depict couples struggling to find the common element of love that will bind them forever. Sometimes they are helped by their own choices, sometimes by circumstances.

-- Sally J. Walker

YULE DOGS OF ENGLAND, 1810

Nine year old Lady Jocelyn Fitzhugh was the Earl of Stafford's littlest child. She knew she owned his heart. She was his only daughter who got her way most of the time. She liked out-smarting her four teenage brothers. The Earl respected that. Her mother didn't. She worried about Josie not being a proper lady in her actions and how she talked.

Everybody was busy somewhere in the house, all except Josie's sleeping nurse, Mrs. Gilmore. Her nurse dozed with snorts and twitches. Instead of reading her lessons, Josie tiptoed from the sitting room. Reaching the hall, the girl raced down the carpet. Only at the corners did she pause. She didn't want to be caught by her mother, one of her brothers, or a servant. She had a plan for this Christmas.

The big manor house needed many people to decorate for the Yuletide party. Everywhere servants hung up holly, ivy, evergreen boughs, red bows, and silver bells. Josie's wish was much more important than all these pretty things. She had made up her mind to change someone's entire future.

MEETING PEOPLE

Josie pushed open the kitchen door. Wonderful smells floated in the air. Orange-glazed goose with stuffing, roast pork with spiced apples, breads, sweets, and Cook's special plum pudding. Josie had to be the one to find the pudding's gold ring. Whoever found it was given a special favor by the Earl. The ring and her father's love would make her plan come true.

"Psst!" she hissed at the boy on a stool in the corner.

He wore thin, drab clothes covered by a really big apron. Eleven-year-old Farrell Rossmore didn't hear her. He carefully shoved whole cloves into oranges taken from the bowl on his lap. The spiced fruit would be baked then dropped into the Wassail punch bowl. The baked oranges would keep the rich drink hot for the grownups. Farrell looked serious about the job given him by Cook. Josie knew the orphan boy took pride in every job anyone gave him.

No one guessed he hated kitchen work, but Josie knew. He only wanted to work in the kennels. He only wanted to care for her father's prize fox hounds. Thinking about the dogs made Josie giggle.

Farrell heard that and looked up. He waved, glanced to see if anyone noticed, then went back to his oranges.

"Lady Jocelyn!" Cook called out, her cheeks as round and red as the apples she peeled. "Come get that treat I promised."

Josie knew she should walk across the room like a lady but her heart skipped, so she did, too. Several of the kitchen workers called out Yuletide's greetings. Cook clapped her hands and glared at them. That sent them back to their work.

A bushy white brow arched at Josie. Cook's eyelid slowly winked. She handed a mince tart to the girl. "Now isn't that the finest plum pudding, child?" she asked. A finger pointed at the dark, heavy round cake sitting on its special platter. When Josie nodded, Cook bent closer to whisper, "The gold ring sits right under that sprig of holly. Pushed it in there myself. Ask your father for that piece. You hold up the ring and the Earl will give you what you ask. It's a fine thing for him to do every Christmas Eve, don't you think?"

Josie bit her lip to stop a laugh. "Can Farrell walk me to the kennels?"

"The earl's daughter *asking* for a servant's time? O, child, don't let your mother hear that."

"Or Mrs. Gilmore!" Josie rolled her eyes. She then spoke up loud enough for everybody in the kitchen to hear her. "Cook, I need Farrell to stop this kitchen work to escort me on my afternoon walk. Mrs. Gilmore is napping. And . . . he will need a mince tart, too."

"Of course, Lady Jocelyn," Cook said with a wink. "Well done," she whispered as Farrell's bowl clattered onto the work table.

A December wind blew into the kennels. Farrell added a blanket around the outside of the whelping box. The special box was for the mama dogs and their babies. Josie squatted on her heels. Her dress, petticoats, and coat covered her legs, protecting them from the cold wind.

She stretched to watch the litter of eight fat, black and white puppies nursing at their mother's belly.

"You're sure that will keep them warm?"

"They're dogs, not babies!" Farrell groaned with disgust.

"But they are baby dogs!"

For a long moment the two smiling children watched. Three of the puppies wiggled away. They tumbled over the others trying to get back in place. Their mother raised her head, flicked a tongue over her nearest baby then returned to sleep. She ignored the tiny whimpers and grunts.

"Marta is a good mother, isn't she?" Josie asked.

"She is, but it is more important that she is good on the hunt. She runs hard. She is never fooled by the canny fox. She leads the pack more often than she follows."

Josie wrinkled her nose. "And how would you know all that, Mr. Smarty Pants. You've never gone a'bugling with Mr. Richards."

The boy's face looked hopeful. "No, but Mr. Richards told me all about it. He said I've the touch. He said someday I, too, will be Master of Hound. I might take his place when your father says he's too old. Someday, yes, someday I will train my own pack."

Tears rose to Josie's eyes. She blinked hard and studied the puppies again. "If you were to choose the best of this litter, which one would you ask my father to keep?"

"Morna, the one pushing the others out of the way. She's a strong one."

"Morna? You've named one of them?"

Farrell blushed. He stood to shift the blanket. "Doesn't hurt, does it? Not that the earl would pay any attention to my naming her. He doesn't even know *my* name."

"Morna. Did you know the names of the puppies always begin with same letter as their mother's name? So that one would be Morna of Stafford's Dormer. Dormer was the papa wasn't he?"

Farrell nodded then cocked his head. "Big name for such a little thing."

Their laughter awakened Marta. She smelled and licked several of the puppies.

The village carolers held mugs of Wassail, the thanks for their singing on the manor steps. Josie slipped around the adults filling the hall. She was supposed to stay on the staircase and not bother anyone. She hoped her brothers and Mrs. Gilmore didn't see her before she reached her father. Dressed in his black and white fancy clothes, he talked with his best friend, Thomas Bascom, the Earl of Warton.

She knew they talked about their kennels. The two men liked to compare their dogs. Both estates were known for their wonderful dogs. People came to them from all over England to buy, breed, or train with either the Stafford or Warton hounds.

"William, my Gentry has fathered the best litters this year. Wonderful promise. In fact, I brought over an especially nice male I've named Clarion. Different coloring. Hope his voice can live up to his name!"

"By Jove, your pride is too much!" Josie's father teased. "Did your footman take him to the kitchens?"

The Earl of Warton's laugh boomed. The two men looked around like plotting schoolboys. Warton clamped a hand on her father's shoulder. "How did you guess? Let's have a look before your dear wife calls all to the plum pudding!"

Josie followed them to the kitchen. She stayed close to the wall so they wouldn't see her. Her father's laugh and good mood warmed her heart. In the kitchen she found the two men nodding and smiling at the scene before them.

The Warton footman sat on the corner stool. He held a meat pie in his hand. Farrell knelt beside the stool, petting a young, skinny black and white hound. Every black spot was perfectly outlined in brown. Josie had never seen such a beautiful dog. And no one, including the two earls, had ever seen such a young dog behaving so well. Farrell did have the touch.

"Clarion!" Farrell spoke firmly. The floppy ears perked. "Sit!" The animal dropped to his behind. The boy held up one finger then slowly moved it up, down, up, down. "Clarion, speak!" A weak effort turned into a small-throated bugle.

The entire kitchen staff, the earls, and Josie applauded loudly. Both boy and dog jumped, startled from their shared efforts. Farrell blushed. Clarion wet on Cook's shiny clean floor.

"Well done, boy." William Fitzhugh patted the boy's back. "You are Farrell Rossmore, aren't you? Mr. Richards says good things about you. I see he is right."

The low flames lit the plum pudding on the table before the Earl of Stafford.

"Ladies and gentlemen, boys and girls, please be up-standing with your eggnog. I toast to the happiness of the Yule season and . . . to dogs a'bugling on Christmas Eve!"

"William, please stop talking about dogs at the table," Josie's mother groaned.

Josie held her breath as the pudding cake was covered to put out the flames. Her father held up the knife and looked directly at his favorite child.

"And where do you want your piece cut, Josie?"

"At the holly, Papa. Please."

She wiggled in her seat staring at the pudding on the plate before her. Why did they have to wait until everyone had their piece? Even if they all wanted to see who had the ring, she already knew. Above the table's merry noise, her mother rang the bell to signal the start. Only forks on plates sounded.

Josie wasted no time. Her fork hit metal. She lifted the gold ring between two fingers. "I got the ring, Papa!"

"She cheated!" her brother Samuel called out. His mother glared at him. He looked at his brothers who only shook their heads.

MEETING PEOPLE

The earl almost smiled then looked serious. "What is the boon you ask of me?"

Josie pushed her chair back and marched to her father's chair, her head high. "The Earl of Warton gifted you with Clarion, Papa. I want him."

"Well-well, now—"

"I'm not done, Papa."

"I see. Go on, Josie."

"And I want one of Marta's puppies. I've already picked her out."

"Her?"

"Yes, a girl and she will be named Morna of Stafford's Dormer. Morna means 'dearly loved.' I asked."

"I see. I have a feeling there is more."

Her knees felt shaky. She wasn't certain if he would grant this part of her wish. "And I want to give Morna and Clarion of Warton's Gentry to Farrell Rossmore, so he can be Master of Hound of his own pack . . . ah, someday. Then he won't be just an unknown orphan boy."

Her father blinked. He looked up at his wife who dabbed at her eyes with her napkin. He then looked at Thomas Bascom who nodded.

"Well, Josie, I see you understand the spirit of the Yule season. Better to give than receive. Consider your wishes granted! I believe young Rossmore is in the kitchen with his new hound. Go tell him the news, but . . . walk like a young lady."

Of course, she didn't.

--The End--

YULE DOGS OF ENGLAND, 1810
GLOSSARY

a'bugling or bugle – loud howling sound instead of a bark made by some kinds of dogs.

boon – a gift or wish made real.

bough – a tree limb.

Earl – an English title given to the head of a rich family and passed on to his oldest son.

estate – a lot of land owned by one family.

footman – a male servant.

kennel – a place where dogs are kept.

manor – a very big house.

mince – fruit filling made of apples, raisins, and spices.

nurse – a person put in charge of young children in a rich home.

orphan – a person or child with both parents dead and usually no other family.

plum pudding – a heavy Christmas cake with alcohol poured over it and set afire when served.

proper – well mannered, an expected way to act.

MEETING PEOPLE

respect – look up to, admire.

servant – a person who works for someone.

Wassail – a punch made with apple cider, alcohol, and spices served at Christmas.

whelping – female dog giving birth.

Yule or Yuletide – another way to say Christmas.

YULE DOGS OF ENGLAND, 1810
MENTOR QUESTIONS

Q1. What was the holiday being celebrated in the story? What were most of the servants doing? Why do you think it took so many people?

Q2. Why do you think Josie was her father's favorite child? Do you think some of the servants agreed? Why or Why not?

Q3. What worried Josie's mother? Do you think that bothered Josie? Why or why not?

Q4. Who was Josie's special friend? Why do you think he was living there? What was he doing in the kitchen? What would happen to the oranges?

Q5. What was the holiday dish Cook had made and what had she done with it to help Josie?

Q6. What interest did Josie share with her friend? Why did he know more about that than Josie? What had he done on his own? How do you think that helped Josie and her plan?

Q7. What were the dogs raised for? What sound did this kind of dog make? What was the title of the man who took care of the dogs? Who has he to Josie's friend?

Q8. The man from next door gave Josie's father a dog. When he hoped the dog lived up to his name, what do you think "Clarion" means?

Q9. What did Josie do with the ring? Why were her father and mother proud of her?

Q10. How do you think Farrell's life changed after the story?

YULE DOGS OF ENGLAND, 1810
POSSIBLE ANSWERS

A1. It was Christmas. Sometimes in England Christmas is also called Yuletide. The servants were decorating the big house. The manor house was so big all of the servants had to help.

A2. Josie was her father's favorite child because she was the youngest, the only girl, and she didn't let her four older brothers boss her around. Cook liked Josie and helped learn to be a lady. She gave her treats and told her where she hid the gold ring to get her wish.

A3. Josie's mother wanted her to act like a lady who walks instead of runs, who stays with her nurse, and who knows how to order around servants. Josie didn't care about any of that. She made up her own mind how she was going to act and talk.

A4. Farrell Rossmore was a boy two years older than Josie who had no parents. Rich people in those times took orphans into their homes as servants. He did whatever work he was told to do but didn't feel sorry for himself. He was sticking cloves into oranges in the kitchen. The oranges would be baked and put into the punch called Wassail to keep it hot.

A5. Cook made a Christmas cake called plum pudding. She showed Josie where she had pushed the gold ring into the cake. Josie had to ask her father for that piece of the cake so she would get the ring. The person who found the ring in the cake could ask the Earl for a gift or favor.

A6. Josie and Farrell liked the dogs raised by the Earl. Farrell mostly worked in the kennels taking care of the dogs so he knew more about them than Josie. He had named one of Marta's puppies which the Earl usually did. He showed he liked that puppy best and Josie knew which puppy she would ask for to give to him.

A7. The hounds were raised to hunt in a pack. These chase foxes. Hounds make a loud howling noise instead of bark. The man in charge of the kennel is called Master of Hound. Mr. Richards was Farrell's boss and was training him how to care for the dogs. He sounds like he was a kind of father to Farrell.

A8. Since the dogs howl loudly and the men liked that sound, "Clarion" must mean something like "loud sounding."

A9. Josie took the ring to her father and asked him for a list of things: the young dog named Clarion just given to him by the neighbor, one of Marta's female puppies, and finally permission to then give the two dogs to Farrell. She wanted him to one day raise and train his own pack of hounds so he would be important and not just an unknown orphan. Josie's parents were proud that she would ask for gifts that would be given to someone else to make their life better.

A10. Possibly Farrell would grow up to take over being the Earl of Stafford's Master of Hound. His Clarion and Morna would have strong puppies that become respected fox hounds that people would want to buy.

A HARD WAY TO GO

A WESTERN

Bill Matting liked the feel of his own sweat. It had better feel good. There was no turning back now. Home was far behind him.

He enjoyed the breeze and the dust. Those things made the trail away from home that much more real.

Everything was new to him, his clothes, his horse, and now this town.

He tied his reins to the saloon hitching rail. Then he let his mind drift back along that sweet trail. Yes, he was travel-tired, but it felt good, didn't it?

He took off his new hat and wiped his sweating brow. Carefully he put the hat back on at an angle. Then he took a deep breath.

The town around him was not too different from home. It wasn't much of a place. It was too small for his liking. But it was new, and that's what counted. Here people would meet the new Bill Matting.

Bill decided to start with a beer. Suddenly his chest hurt. He felt guilty. One beer, even a first one, couldn't hurt, he told himself. Beer was supposed to wet your thirst. It was supposed to take the edge off a man's worries. Bill was sure someone had said that sometime. And a beer wasn't hard liquor.

The saloon doors swung in. They squeaked loudly as he walked through them. He liked to hear his spurs jingle as he walked across the wooden floor. He was pleased that his boot heels made his steps sound solid and certain. They sounded like a man's walk in a man's place.

The late afternoon sun lit up a small part of the wood floor. The rest of the room was shadowed. The dust on the big mirror behind the bar dulled the light. It wasn't the cleanest place he had ever seen. At least it was a little cooler inside than on the street. It would be even cooler after his drink, Bill thought.

A chair squeaked in the dimness to his right. The three men sitting at a table were cowboys, by the look of their clothes. They played cards. He could tell it was a game of poker. The men didn't look away from their cards to notice him.

Bill looked around the place more carefully. He was alone with the three poker players. Could one of them be the bartender? He didn't know if h should call out for service or just pound on the bar top.

He didn't have long to worry about what to do. The curtained doorway to his left parted and a bald man came through. He wore an apron and carried a small crate of bottles.

"Ah, there you are!" Bill slapped the bar. His words were a little too loud for the small room.

The man set down the crate then stood up slowly. "Well?" he said. "Do you want something, cowboy? Or are you hanging around with that bunch? I've got supplies to unload."

Bill drew his shoulders back. "You keep your nose out of my business. Just worry about your own, mister. I'll take a big wet one."

"A big wet what?"

"Why, a beer!"

"Ohhhhh, of course." The bartender grabbed a mug. He filled the glass and slammed it down in front of Bill.

Bill rolled his hands on the glass before lifting the mug to his lips. He just managed to control a choke. He had always thought beer would taste like apple cider. It didn't.

"Hey, barkeep! Bring us three beers!"

The voice sounded like someone Bill knew. He looked in the dirty mirror and saw the table behind him. He tried to pick out the man who had spoken. Sure enough, that was Cal Rogers.

With beer in hand, Bill called out loudly, "Cal Rogers, you old dog, you! What're you doing in this town?"

Three sun-darkened faces look up.

The youngest man at the table turned his head. He narrowed his eyes. "Is it any of your business, boy?"

Bill felt his face redden. He laughed and moved from one foot to another. The men at the table looked tense. When they looked at Bill, their faces seemed to say "Not welcome."

MEETING PEOPLE

"Well . . . I . . .," Bill started to speak. "Don't you remember . . . Millsville? I'm Bill Matting. You know me. We went to school together."

The three men fell back in their chairs, their tension gone.

A broad smile slid easily across Cal's lips. "Sure, kid, I remember. Your old man had that good-for-nothing dirt farm south of town." With his empty hand, Cal waved toward a chair. "Come on. Join us. This is Roy Bob Jeffries and that's Les Crawford. Fellas, this is an old friend of the family."

The bartender came to the table with a tray of three beers.

The man called Les grabbed one off the tray. "What family?" Les laughed at his own joke then raised his glass to drink half the yellow liquid in one swallow.

Cal didn't even look at Les. He looked at Jeffries, glanced at Bill sitting in the last chair at their table then again looked at Jeffries. Bill could tell Jeffries was their leader and Cal looked worried about what the man thought of him joining them.

Jeffries moved like a careful, slow cat. With his eyes half closed, he studied Bill. Bill moved in his chair. He knew the man could see he was a farm boy-turned-cowboy. Bill smiled back then took a long drink of his beer like he was used to all this. He nodded to Jeffries then Les before looking into Cal's eyes.

"Yes, sir, Bill." Call nodded. "I see you finally made it away from that poor town and your Bible-banging pa of yours. What are you doing lately? Working as a cowboy?"

"Sure he is!" Les laughed then downed the last of his beer.

Bill leaned back in his chair trying not to care. "Yeah, I just finished up over at the . . . the Bar-X at Kiley."

"Bar-X? I know Biggs, the foreman. A real hard man," Jeffries said.

Bill took another sip of his drink to wet his suddenly dry throat. "Oh, yeah. Sure is."

The three poker players watched the bartender leave through the curtain.

"Say, let's get back to our poker, Roy Bob." Les pushed Jeffries' arm. "We need to be moving on,"

"Shut your mouth, Les." Jeffries gave him a mean glance.

Bill took a bigger gulp of his beer. He shut his eyes at the bitter taste. When he opened his eyes, he saw Jeffries motion toward the door to the street.

Cal nodded at his boss.

Bill looked harder at the shadows by the door. Gear had been piled there.

"How about joining in a couple of hands of poker, kid?" Jeffries asked.

Bill felt warmth grow in his gut and flow up to his chest. He grinned at Jeffries. "The name's Bill, not kid," he said. "Sure, I'll play. That is real friendly of you to invite me."

"What are you doing, Roy Bob?" Les asked. His tone said he didn't like it.

Jeffries pointed a warning finger. "Deal a new hand, Les." The friendliness he had shown Bill turned cold. He stared down Les's question.

MEETING PEOPLE

The smaller man looked away. Then he asked, "Is Five-Card Stud all right with you, kid?"

Bill grinned. "That's my best game. And, like I said, my name is Bill." He drank the last of his beer. Looking around the table, he saw Jeffries wink at Cal. Well, Bill thought, I'll just show these men how to play cards.

Les gave out the cards.

Cal left the table to fill the four empty mugs at the deserted bar. As he set them back on the table he said, "This round's on me, fellas."

Jeffries looked over his cards. "Bill, the chips cost one dollar each. You have to put in two chips to play each game. And you can't bet less than two chips as the betting goes around."

Cal nodded at Bill before sitting down and taking up his own cards. He saw Cal wink at Jeffries and the older man nod.

In his head, Bill counted the money he still had. He had bought the clothes, saddle, and pony. He thought he had forty-three dollars left. He wouldn't lose the hard-earned money. These men didn't know how well he played cards. He had always been lucky in any kind of game, but Five-Card Stud topped the list. "I can stand the cost. Give me forty dollars worth of chips."

Bill put on his blank poker face so the other players would not read any signs of what he held in cards. His first hand included a pair of jacks.

No one looked up as each man put in his two chips to play. The players asked for the second cards. Dealer Les handed them out.

Bill came up with another jack out of his three new cards. He was so happy he nearly dumped his second beer. He looked around the table. When he stretched out his legs, he let his spurs dig into the wood floor. He waited for the bets to start. Calmly he listened to the big wall clock ticking. He had time.

The first pot was his! Not a word was spoken as he pulled the pile of chips to him. Everyone threw their two chips to the center of the scarred table to start the second game. Cards were given out. His cards this time were even better. He had a pair of fours and a pair of aces. He almost smiled at his two pairs, but didn't. He had to stay calm.

Bill let the bets go around two times before making his move to raise big. "I'll raise eight," he stated. Coolly he counted out his chips in a single stack. He carefully placed the stack in the center of the table.

Jeffries raised an eyebrow. "Oh, yeah?"

"I'm out of the game, Bill. I know you aren't betting that much for nothing." Cal winked at Bill.

Les Crawford moved his cards in his hand and sat forward to stare at them. "Well, I haven't got it so bad myself. I'll raise your bet by another four chips."

Jeffries shrugged. "I guess we all have a touch of Lady Luck today. I'll see that, Les, and raise another four chips."

Bill's stomach tightened. He smiled and tossed in the needed sixteen chips. Without smiling, he counted out more. "And I'll raise eight more."

Les frowned at his cards. He looked from Bill to Jeffries. He then stared hard at his cards as if that would make something change.

Cal swished the beer left in his mug. "Getting kind of deep for you, Les?" he teased.

"I've told you before to shut your smart mouth," Les snapped. He looked at his cards again. "Naw. I'm out." Angry, he threw his cards down then shoved away from the table.

Jeffries laughed. "Okay, Bill. It's just you and me. So, I'll see that and raise my last ten dollars."

Bill licked his dry lips. Fourteen dollars was all he had left. He took a deep gulp of his fresh beer. "Well . . . here. That's fourteen." He pushed the chips into the growing pile.

Jeffries sat forward. He turned his eyes from his cards to Bill and back by way of Cal. "Now, boy, I'm out of money. How about trusting me? Old Cal knows me. He'll—"

Cal hit the table with his palm. The blow sounded loud in the room's quiet. Everybody looked at him. "Roy Bob, you got that extra saddle with our pack by the front door." He pointed his thumb at the doorway.

Bill looked at the shadows again. He saw the carved leather of a saddle's skirt. Most of the saddle lay hidden by saddle bags, bed rolls, and other gear carelessly dumped out of the way.

Bill thought of the worn saddle he had bought for ten dollars. The old saddle came with the old horse tied to the hitching rail out front.

It wasn't much of a decision. Bill shrugged for show. "I've got a saddle but I'll take it . . . if you want to call my hand, Roy Bob."

"Wait a minute, Bill. That saddle is worth more than all the money you put in that pile."

Again, Bill shrugged as if he didn't care.

"Aw, Roy Bob, you don't need it. Anyway, don't you have a good hand there?" Cal teased the older man.

"Of course I do!" Jeffries drained his beer. "Okay, kid, I'll bet that saddle. What have you got?"

"Two pair," Bill smiled and flipped his five cards onto the table in a fan shape.

"Oh, no!" Jeffries groaned. He threw his cards down showing three queens.

Les laughed and pounded on the bar top. His actions drew a mean glare from Jeffries.

Total joy and manly pride glowed through the buzzing in Bill's head. He swept the chips into his new hat.

Cal slapped him on the back. "Well, old friend, that bartender will be back soon. He'll trade you cash for those chips."

"And I'll leave the saddle there by the door. We have to be on the trail before dark," Jeffries added, looking sad. He shook his head and sighed.

As the older man turned, Les grabbed his arm. "You aren't really--"

Jeffries lifted Les's hand. He gritted his teeth as he spoke, "I said we're moving on. Get that gear out the door and back on our horses. Now!" Les stepped away from him. Jeffries turned to Bill. "Kid, I mean, Bill, you played a man's hand. Maybe another game, another day."

MEETING PEOPLE

Bill couldn't hold back his grin. "I'll count on it, Roy Bob."

Cal slapped him on the back. "I'll be seeing you somewhere along the trail, Bill. You enjoy that saddle. You deserve a prize like that for all you lived through as a kid." He grabbed the last set of saddlebags and bedroll. He waved his hand then followed his two friends out the saloon's swinging doors.

"I do deserve it," Bill said to himself as he stared at the saddle. "Barkeep! Hey, barkeep!" he called, pounding the bar top until the bald man came back into the room.

"Did your friends leave, boy?"

"We're hitting the trail, if it's any business of yours . . . which it isn't." Bill's words slurred. He spilled the chips from his hat onto the bar. "I'm paying for the beers out of these chips. Cash them in while I take that new saddle out to my horse."

The bartender's eyes narrowed. He gritted his teeth as he replied, "Oh, yes, sir."

His mean tone of voice didn't lessen Bill's joy. He smiled as he put his hat back on.

Bill swayed as he lifted the heavy saddle. He carried it through the doors. He tripped down the two steps to the hitching rail. Sunlight flashed off the silver trim on the saddle, making him blink.

As Bill stumbled forward, his surprised horse pulled back on his tied reins. "Here now, Red," Bill warned the silly horse. When he dropped the saddle into the dust of the street, the horse jumped. "Stand still there!"

He flipped the stirrup up and over the worn seat of the saddle on the horse's back. His fingers worked to undo the cinch of the old saddle. The horse blew a snort of relief as he slid the old saddle off. Bill stroked the horse's shoulder before he settled the saddle blanket back in place. "This new saddle won't improve your looks, horse, but it will improve mine."

"Howdy, son."

Bill looked up. The sunlight made his eyes water. He wiped at them to better see who talked to him. A short, thin man stood at the saloon door.

"Howdy," Bill replied. He was afraid he'd had too many beers. The bright sun now made his head hurt.

"New in town?"

"Just passing through."

"Yeah, not many folks like it here. Drifters like you mostly keep moving. And that's good for us." The man turned to enter the saloon. He almost ran into the bartender. That man was on his way out with Bill's winnings.

"Howdy, Tom," the little man greeted the bartender.

"Hello there, Marshal," the bartender said. "What are you doing here? I thought you were out at the Anders ranch."

"I was. He's dead all right. He was killed as he got home with his payroll."

Bill grunted as he swung the new saddle into place on top of the old saddle blanket.

"Hardworking men aren't safe these days. Do you know who killed him?" the bartender asked.

"Funny thing about that, Tom. They shot his horse out from under him."

"Well, that's not so funny."

"Naw, I didn't mean it like that. See, they didn't just take his payroll and leave. They also stripped his horse of that fancy saddle. You remember him showing it off. It had all that carving in the leather and the silver wrappings."

Bill stopped in the middle of tightening the cinch. He stood tall. His shoulders tensed. He felt cold sober as he glanced at the two men in the saloon doorway.

His movement had the marshal looking back at him. The lawman raised his eyes to the old horse.

Bill's hands were sweaty. They rested on top of an easily won fancy saddle.

-- The End --

A HARD WAY TO GO
GLOSSARY

bartender (barkeep or barkeeper) – a person who serves drinks in a bar or saloon.

breeze – a soft wind.

buzzing -- a ringing in the ears or unclear thinking.

carved – cut into patterns or designs.

cinch – leather strap that goes under the horse's belly to hold a saddle in place.

cowboy -- someone who works with cattle and horses on a ranch.

curtain – cloth that hangs down to cover a doorway or window.

darn or darned – a mild swear word or cuss word.

deserted – no one around.

fellas – fellows, men.

foreman – boss man.

glare -- a harsh stare when someone is angry or doesn't like something.

grab – take hold with a hand.

MEETING PEOPLE

gritted (teeth) – jaws or teeth tight as if in pain or anger.

hard-earned – lots of work done to get something or money.

hitching rail – a wooden bar used to tie up horses in front of places.

howdy – a cowboy way of saying hello.

liquor – drinks (not beer) made with strong alcohol.

marshal – lawman for a town.

mirror – a piece of glass with paint on its back used to show a person what he or she looks like.

mug – a thick glass cup with a handle.

narrow – smaller, thinner than before.

naw – a way of saying "no."

payroll – the list of people working for someone or the money the owner pays the hired workers.

people – men, women, children.

poker – a card game in which people bet to see which players have the best combination of cards.

saddle – a seat for a person to sit atop a horse with stirrups for the person's feet, usually made of leather and held on the horse by a cinch.

saddlebags -- cloth or leather sacks or bags that are tied behind the saddle and hang down each side of the horse to contain the rider's things.

saloon – a bar with drinks, food, and grown-up fun in the Old West.

shrug – raise or lift the shoulders, meaning "I don't care."

slurred – unclear or run together spoken words.

sober – not drunk.

spur – a piece of metal worn on a boot heel and held in place by a leather strap around a cowboy's boot, used to touch the horse's sides to make him go faster. Called spurs in paired set.

stirrup – The part of the saddle where the rider puts a foot.

stumble – trip or walk unevenly.

tense – feeling worried or uneasy shown by tightening muscles.

worth – value of something in cost or meaning.

yeah – a way of saying "yes."

youngest – age is less than others.

MEETING PEOPLE

A HARD WAY TO GO
MENTOR QUESTIONS

Q1. From the clues in the story, what do you know about Bill? What do you know about the other men playing cards in the saloon?

Q2. At first, how did Bill feel about winning the saddle?

Q3. Do you think Bill won the saddle on his own? Why or why not?

Q4. Do you think Bill was totally aware of what was going on in the saloon? Why or why not?

Q5. Why do you think Cal and his two friend left the saloon before dark?

Q6. What happened at the Anders ranch?

Q7. As Bill was changing the saddle and listening to the bartender and marshal, what ideas came to his mind?

Q8. Who do you think was (or were) the big winner (s) in this story and why?

Q9. What do you think the author means by "an easily won saddle"?

Q10. How do you think this story really ends?

A HARD WAY TO GO
POSSIBLE ANSWERS

A1. Bill wants to be a tough guy. He has never had a beer before. He may not be a real cowboy. He wants people to think he is cowboy. He thinks he is a good card player. The cowboys in the saloon were probably killers and robbers. They probably killer Mr. Anders. They probably stole the fancy saddle. They may have wanted to fool into taking the saddle so they weren't caught with it. They didn't really like Bill.

A2. Bill thought he won the saddle because he was a good card player. He thought he beat the other cowboys. He thought he was pretty smart. He was proud of what he thought he had done.

A3. Some readers will probably say the other cowboys let him win to get rid of the fancy saddle. Or maybe make the bartender think Bill was the killer. Hints: The winks between the players, and the way the cowboys seemed to fight over betting with the saddle.

A4. Bill did see the winks. Bill drank at least two beers, but was not used to drinking. Bill was putting on a bit of a show. He was proud of his card skills and of sitting with the cowboys.

A5. Answers may vary. The men probably wanted to be able to ride and hide at night and be gone before the lawmen came back or the crime was known.

A6. Mr. Anders had taken his payroll out. He was killed for the money. His fancy saddle had been stolen because it looked so valuable.

A7. Bill might have realized the stolen saddle was very valuable. He might have thought the lawman and the bartender saw him with the saddle and thought he killed her Anders. He might have thought the bartender saw him with the cowboys and would tell the lawman he was one of the killers.

A8. Some readers may think Bill is the winner because he got the fancy saddle. Some may think the killers were the winners because they got away and left Bill with the saddle.

A9. Bill may not have really won the saddle. The killers may have let him win or cheated to let him win. They didn't all show their cards.

A10. Answers will vary: The marshal might arrest Bill and put him in jail for something he didn't do. The bartender might say Bill was one of the gang because he joined in their card game. Bill might be able to tell the marshal who the killers were. The lawman might believe Bill and let him leave.

DUMB ANIMALS DON'T THINK

A WESTERN

"Do you have to go?"

"No choice."

The mother pushed a lock of gray-brown hair behind her ear. It didn't stay.

She bit her lip, watching her son. He looked at what he was doing. He put a shirt and a pair of socks into the old saddlebags.

"But I need you, Ramey."

"Ma, you can do anything I can. You can even do Pa's work. Anything that needs doing, anyway." He sounded tired.

"Once I could."

His head came up, stopping her. He looked at her. She seemed so small, sitting there beside the stone fireplace. "There isn't anything left for me here. At least this will be a job and money." He had to turn away from her eyes and her tears.

"You don't have the job yet."

He sighed and shook his head. One hand picked up the saddlebags. With the other hand he took the heavy spurs from the table. "Pa left me these, a rope, and the will to try."

"Ramey."

He stopped in the cabin door.

"Take the horse. I'll borrow a mule when I need an animal."

The boy nodded once. Quickly he stepped outside.

The buckskin horse lifted his head from his small pile of hay. The boy walked toward him, but the animal moved away to the other side of the corral.

A big black dog stepped into the boy's path. The dog's tail fanned the air.

"Get out of the way, Billy!" Ramey kicked at the dog but missed. Ears and tail down, the dog followed the boy to the corral.

The horse moved around as Ramey saddled him. More than once the boy had to tell the horse to stand still. Billy sat in one spot. He watched and waited. He shook with excitement. Ramey knew the dog wanted to go hunting. That wouldn't happen today.

Ramey opened the gate. Then he swung himself up into the saddle. The horse started forward. Ramey jerked on the reins and the horse stopped. The boy had made his point so he let up on the reins. He kicked the horse into a trot through the open gate

Ramey didn't bother to close the corral gate. He didn't think of the dog either, until he heard his mother's voice calling, "You, Billy, dog! Get back here!"

The boy just rode down the hill and turned the horse onto the road. Wagon wheels and the feet of many horses and cattle had made the road through the brush. It led away from home.

That afternoon Ramey stood in another ranch yard. In front of him a wooden board rested on two barrels. It made a table for the ranch owner

Ramey moved from one foot to the other. He turned his father's torn and dirty cowboy hat in his hands. More than twenty men stood around the ranch yard. To Ramey, it felt like their eyes made holes through his back.

"You can ride a horse and throw a rope. But do you know much about cattle, boy?" Tom Thompson leaned back from his board table. He rested his shoulders against the wall of the house. With his thumbs in his vest, he tapped his fingers on his big belly.

"Well, sir, after the war, my pa started me chasing steers out of the brush for him. There was enough to keep us fed."

The old rancher frowned. He looked the boy over. "Does that mean you were stealing cows?"

Ramey stuck his chin up. He spoke slowly so the man would know he meant his words. "No, sir. We never took a branded animal. We never killed one, either. Pa was careful about that."

"Tom, I knew Ben Caldwell. Good man. I heard he died two weeks ago. Too bad." Nat Risley folded his arms. He stood to the rancher's right with one foot resting on the porch step. He wore his hat pushed forward, hiding his eyes.

"It's good of you to say that, MrRisley." The boy nodded to him. "That's why I'm here. I have to make my own way, now."

Thompson looked at his trail boss. "Well, Risley?"

"We have a job for $20 a month and food."

"Thank you, sir." Ramey stood tall. He put on his father's old, gray hat.

Risley spit in the dust then wiped his hand across his mouth. "You can thank me when you're eating dust or swimming a flood. Or when you're trying to turn Old Brindle, our lead steer. It's a long way to Kansas, boy."

Thompson wrote in his record book: On 20 April 1870, hired Ramson Caldwell at $20 per month. He turned the book to Ramey and held up his ink pe. nA finger of his other hand pointed at his writing. "Sign here, beside your name."

"Sorry, sir, uh—"

"Just make an X then put your things in the cook's wagon."

Taking great care, Ramey made his X. Risley looked past him to the buckskin. The horse stood quietly with its reins on the ground.

"Is that your only horse?'

"Pa sold the rest."

"On this cattle drive, he joins the horse herd. Anyone can ride him. He's just like any other horse. Does that bother you?"

"No, sir. I don't mind using other animals. My pa taught me animals are to be used by man."

Risley lifted his head so the boy could see his eyes. He stared hard at Ramey. "I remember Ben Caldwell thought well of his animals. He treated a good horse with respect. And he got respect in return."

Ramey smiled. "Well, Mr. Risley, I know Pa's horses did what he wanted. Respect?" He shook his head. "No. That says they think, like they care. That horse doesn't care who rides it. And I don't either."

Ramey nodded to Risley then to Thompson. He walked to his horse to get his saddlebags.

On his second day of work, Ramey got his food at the cook's bean pot. The boy only took two steps before he had the plate close to his mouth. He ate the steaming mess as fast as he could. His second helping was a hunk of warm bread and a tin cup full of coffee. He sat on his heels at the edge of the firelight to finish eating. Near him the other riders ate or talked.

British George poked his fork in the air while bean juice dripped down his arm. "I tell you, boys, that steer is the boss, not our Mister Nat Risley."

"I was riding point today. All I did was sleep in the saddle. That big old steer just grunted. The cattle started moving as if he told them to move." Joe Whitsup liked to make jokes. Two cowboys laughed this time

"Here, here!" British George lifted his coffee cup in a cheer.

Fifty-year-old Grumpy Barnes stood beside Ramey. Grumpy had a bad knee. He never sat until he was ready to lie down for the night. The trail drive was his third with Risley. He cleared his throat. "I'm telling you, Old Brindle knows things. He knows which cow is having its baby and needs to stop. He knows which of the young steers is likely to break away. And he knows which horses he can outrun."

"What a story!" Ramey hissed then took a gulp of coffee.

"The kid thinks we're joking." Whitsup looked around at the other men. "I have five dollars, five whole dollars, do you hear? And I'm betting one of us is going to fall off a horse and run for a tree with Old Brindle chasing him!"

Grumpy laughed. "That's no bet."

Risley stepped up to the fire. "That steer got me on the last drive."

British George slapped his own knee. "Mister Risley, that should give you the right to decide what is a fair bet."

Ramey stood, shaking his head. "I'm getting my bedroll. This is stupid."

The herd moved at a trot, walk, stop, trot again for two weeks. Finally they came to the first river. The horse herd grazed a half mile away from the crowded cattle.

Ramey rode toward the horses. He could hear the river's groaning sound. It ran bank full from rains upriver. The boy got off his horse and worked to take off the saddle.

"Hey, kid," he called over his horse's back.

The horse wrangler was about Ramey's age, but had better manners. His mother had come from the East. She was a school teacher on the ranch where his Mexican father was foreman.

The wrangler slowly walked to Ramey. He didn't stop until the two boys were almost nose to nose. Ramey had little room to swing his saddle to the ground.

"What do you want, boy?" the dark-skinned young man asked.

"You aren't old enough to call me 'boy.'" Ramey poked him in the chest then stared hard into his dark eyes. His look was steady and mean.

The other boy didn't blink. "You learn to call me by name and I'll do the same for you."

"All right, *Senor* Chavez," Ramey said, sounding even more rude. "I need a horse that is a good swimmer."

The wrangler smiled. "I think maybe Mister Ramson Caldwell cannot swim."

Ramey tried to control his anger. He spoke in a flat voice. "I said I need a swimming horse."

The Mexican boy stared for a long moment. "I will rope the big red with the white foot for you."

"He swims?"

"He has a big heart and likes—"

"Can he swim?" Ramey repeated.

"Oh, yes, he can, boy."

MEETING PEOPLE

Risley stood in his stirrups and tried to see down-river. He hoped the rolling river looked better around the bend. It didn't.

Six riders sat in their saddles and waited. They watched the high, fast river water. All of them looked worried.

"This spot shouldn't be deep!" Risley sat down in his saddle so suddenly, his horse jumped. "Joe!" he shouted. "Go cut out Old Brindle and get him up here."

Ramey watched the red-brown water roll up, curl, fade, and rush on. He wiped his hand across his mouth. His voice sounded louder than he wanted. "MrRisley, who is taking him across?"

The trail boss glanced at him. Then he looked back at the far bank downstream. "Whitsup for one. Maybe—"

"I want to do it."

Risley looked at Ramey more closely. "He isn't easy, boy."

"So I heard, but I still want to try."

"You're riding a swimmer. That'll help." Risley nodded

Ramey turned to look at the clear spot in the trees. That's where the herd would walk through behind Old Brindle. The big steer would start and the rest would follow.

The river's noise was loud. The cattle beyond the trees were even louder. For a moment Ramey thought of the big animals and their long horns. He thought of them fighting in the water. He thought of them moving close, pulling him under. He felt sick. If he went in the water first with just Old Brindle, he would have a chance.

Whitsup and Grumpy rode away from the trees. They flapped their ropes, driving the angry old steer in front of them. Ramey kicked his horse with his spurs. He rode forward to meet the two riders. His shaking hand worked the loop of his rope.

The huge steer stopped, bellowed, and started to turn back. The riders circled him. Horses snorted. Men yelled.

Whitsup roped the nearest horn. Old Brindle's horns were about eight feet long from tip to tip. The cowboy flipped his rope across the steer's head. He flipped it again, harder and wider. It caught around the other horn. He made several passes back and forth in front of the upset steer. Finally he got the loops tight around the base of the long horns.

Again and again Ramey tried to rope the steer's horns from his side. He couldn't get it. Grumpy jumped from his horse. He picked up the boy's loop from the dirt. In one toss he had the loop over a horn. The old rider was back in the saddle by the time the steer swung those horns at him.

Ramey rode in front of the steer. He tried to copy Whitsup and catch the other horn. The steer shook his head up and down. He backed. Whitsup couldn't keep his rope tight and out of Ramey's way. He couldn't pull the steer's head enough for Ramey to get his rope tight.

Old Brindle didn't like any of it. He ran for the river. The ropes pulled the two cowboys and their horses with him. The boy didn't have time to think. Cowboys and horses hit the river water along with the angry steer.

Ramey's horse didn't go all the way under. The boy let go of the reins. One shaking hand grabbed the saddle horn. The other held Old Brindle's rope.

MEETING PEOPLE

The next moment the cold water came up to Ramey's shoulders. The swimming horse lifted him. Water sounds filled Ramey's ears. He saw Whitsup ahead of him. The older cowboy was on the other side of the eight-foot horns. In between them, the steer's wide nose blew a spray of water as the animal fought the river.

Something pulled at Ramey's hip. His swimming horse turned, moving up against steer. Big tree roots flashed by the boy's face. His horse bucked and screamed above the river's roar. Ramey dug his feet into the stirrups to hold on. The horse twisted to get away from the tree-thing.

A wave of water lifted the men, horses, steer, and tree. The water dropped away. In that moment the ropes tangled.

Ramey saw the other cowboys trotting along the bank. They were too far away to help.

A roll of water slammed into his back, pushing him from the saddle. He rolled across the steer's boney cowhide. His rope snapped. He went under the water. Mud filled his mouth. Fear ripped through him. Ramey swung his arms wide. His hand brushed the cowhide and landed on a horn. He grabbed it to pull himself above the water and suck in a breath. He wrapped his whole arm around the horn. His other hand grabbed a handful of the animal's neck hair.

The steer swam easily to shore. The animal stumbled then jumped in the climb up the bank. The boy held on.

Feeling solid ground under his boots, Ramey let go of horn and hide. He rolled to the side. He got out of the way just as Old Brindle topped the bank. The boy lay very still, his eyes clamped shut, his heart pounding.

His shaking body pressed into the hard ground under him. He could hear leaves moving above him and the river beyond. Remembering the steer, he blinked open his eyes.

Somehow he found the power to jump to his feet. He ran to the nearest tree. His muddy fingers and wet boots scraped at the bark like the claws of a weak bear cub. He couldn't get up the tree, but there was no need. Old Brindle just stood on the bank, his sides moving in and out with each breath. He kept his head down while his black eyes watched the boy.

"Hey, you, Brindle! Get out of here!" Whitsup yelled as he rode up on his wet horse. His flapping arms sprayed red-brown water drops

The steer tipped his horns and trotted off. He passed Ramey as if he didn't see him.

"I thought he'd kill you," Whitsup said as he stepped out of his saddle beside the tree.

"I did, too." Ramey turned to stare after the steer.

The sounds of the river, yelling men, and the swimming herd filled the air.

No rain fell during the next two weeks. One night dark clouds rolled over the sky. Thunder crashed. Sheets of lightning lit up the backs and horns of the milling herd. The scared cattle stampeded. They ran and spread out over miles of open land.

When it was all over, the cowboys split up. They rode off to find the missing cattle. Ramey and Grumpy went with British George. They found only fifty cows in their swing to the west of the trail.

They were out two days with only a few rabbits to eat. British George wanted to kill and cut up one of the steers. Grumpy and Ramey said no. Thinking about the good meal at camp, they headed back to the herd. The bored cattle and tired horses didn't like moving at a trot.

Ramey's buckskin horse tripped over a rock. Looking down, the boy saw the tracks. He stopped and got off his horse to look at the trail. He knew they were made by Old Brindle's wide hooves. The tracks led off into a narrow, winding gully that had to lead to a canyon. He thought the steer had probably smelled water back in there

"Grumpy!" Ramey shouted. He waved the old rider over and pointed at the tracks. "As big as those are that has to be Old Brindle."

Grumpy nodded. He turned his horse back to the fifty head of cattle moving north.

Ramey grabbed the reins of Grumpy's horse. "Aren't we going to pick him up?"

"No need."

"What?"

"Boy, let's get going. That old steer will come in tomorrow or the next day. He's like a lost dog that finds its way home. He'll make it back to the herd on his own."

"You're wrong, old man." Ramey stepped into his stirrup and settled back in his saddle. "That steer isn't some trained circus animal. And he doesn't think!"

The boy spurred his horse to follow the tracks into the gully.

Grumpy spit into a print left by the steer.

Ramey heard noises coming from the other side of a big rock. The noises sent a shiver down his back. His buckskin horse bucked and tried to turn around. The animal didn't want to go forward. Ramey jerked the reins and used his spurs to make him keep going.

The trail ended in a high-walled box canyon. The only way out was where Ramey came in. The canyon had become a trap for the steer he followed.

Old Brindle didn't see Ramey. With head and horns down, the animal backed to the far rock wall. He was a long way from the opening where Ramey fought with his upset horse. Those big horns swept side to side.

In front of the steer two thin coyotes paced, growled, and yipped. One jumped forward at Old Brindle. The horns swung. The coyote rolled backwards in the dust. It hit the other coyote. Mean growling and snapping followed. The two coyotes bit at each other. One lost its balance and sat back on its behind. It shook its head from side to side. The other fell toward the steer.

"Mad coyotes! They have rabies," Ramey whispered.

The steer bellowed. The coyote near him stopped, its head wobbling as if was dizzy. For a moment it seemed not to see the big steer then it growled and backed away. It kept backing toward the boy and his upset horse.

The boy reached back and down into his saddlebag for his hand gun. Twisted in the saddle, he had a hard time holding the reins. The scared horse would not stop.

MEETING PEOPLE

It did not want to be there with that coyote getting closer. Ramey's hand wrapped around the Colt gun holding down his clothes. Just then Old Brindle roared like a bull ready to charge. The horse reared up on its back legs.

Ramey rolled backward out of the saddle. As he fell, he heard the horse running back the way they had come. Then his head hit the ground and all sound faded. He fought to think. He had been left to face the animals in that canyon. He shook the hurt from his head as he pushed to sit up.

Turning, he looked right into two red eyes, the eyes of the closest coyote. It jumped at his arm. Knife-like teeth bit into him. The animal growled and yanked, pulling at his arm bone.

Ramey still held the Colt in his right hand. He raised the gun and brought it down hard on the coyote's thin, furry head. The biting teeth let up.

Quickly, the boy pulled his arm free. He aimed the gun and fired. The coyote's body lifted and dropped. The sound of the gunshot bounced off the rock walls.

The coyote's red eyes stayed open. Its bloody tongue flopped over its curled lips. Bubbles of spit slid over its bared teeth.

Ramey got to his knees. He hugged his bleeding arm against his stomach. Fighting the pain, he rocked back and forth. He blinked to clear away the dust Old Brindle kicked up.

The big steer spun and kicked, trying to get rid of the gray thing on its back. The other coyote bit and held on. The steer's long horns couldn't reach it. Old Brindle's breath blew out in long grunts. He sounded tired.

The coyote clawed for a better hold, digging bloody lines down the steer's side. Then it ripped harder at the hide in its mouth. Blood ran from the wounds.

Brindle spun. The coyote swung, his teeth holding the hide as it tore. The tip of one horn rammed into the coyote's soft belly. The steer lifted the yipping animal high. He then threw it into the air. The bleeding coyote landed in the dust and jumped to its feet. It started back toward the steer. Brindle pawed the ground once. The coyote stopped with its legs spread wide. Snapping at the air, it cocked its head. Bubbles of spit and blood fell from the coyote's mouth.

Ramey stood up. "Oh, no, you don't," he groaned.

The coyote didn't see him coming. It didn't see the gun. From six feet away, Ramey fired. The gunshot tore away the coyote's chest. The animal fell forward. Its neck stretched out on the ground with its back end in the air. It flopped onto its side and lay still.

Ramey didn't miss a step. He walked until he stood to one side of Old Brindle. Both of the boy's arms hung at his sides. Blood dripped from his free hand as he held the heavy gun in the other. He planted his feet far apart, but still swayed.

The boy and the steer looked at one another.

Ramey could see the fear and fight drain from the animal's eyes. The red glow of anger faded, too. He wondered if Old Brindle could see the fear in his human eyes. He tried to swallow.

"Those two are dead. That doesn't do us any good," Ramey said sadly. "We can't leave. Not now. We've both got rabies, you know." The steer winked slowly. He did seem to know. "Well, old man, we have to get this over, you and me."

Ramey saw Old Brindle frown as the gun roared.

Before he had time to change his mind, the boy put the end of the gun in his own mouth.

"I don't think it's fair," Lee Bledsoe said as he looked around at the other two cowboys he rode with.

"Shut up, Bledsoe. You bet your money along with the rest of us." Whitsup rode beside him, leading Ramey's buckskin horse.

"Risley makes three or four times more than any of us. Just because he bet against the kid--" Bledsoe stopped as Whitsup turned to stare him down.

Grumpy Barnes spit into the dirt. "Maybe I'll collect some money on you, Bledsoe. I can't remember you ever roping that old steer."

"No, and this wasn't my choice, either. I just caught the kid's horse as it ran by me with its empty saddle. And Risley made me come." Bledsoe looked unhappy.

"Is this the one, Grumpy?" Risley called. He had ridden ahead. His hand pointed to a narrow gully.

"That's it."

Half an hour passed as they slowly rode single-file toward the dead-end canyon.

Whitsup broke the silence. "Brindle must have found water since he didn't come back. Don't you think, Mr. Risley?"

"It could be. He always came back before, but he's getting old. And he's getting meaner, too. There's no telling what he's thinking."

"I know what that kid is thinking about. His stomach!" Grumpy Barnes laughed. He lifted his hat to wipe his sleeve across his forehead.

"Or how to get out of a tree," Whitsup called out.

"From the looks of this place, he more likely spent the night on a rock." Risley looked around at the rocky walls of the winding path they followed.

Risley rode into the wider canyon first and stopped. Grumpy's horse pushed him forward and the other two riders crowded in.

"Oh, no!" Grumpy whispered.

The early morning sun only lit up part of the canyon, but the riders could see what they had to. Flies buzzed over four bodies.

Bledsoe coughed and asked, "What happened?"

No one answered. They all got down off their horses. Bledsoe held the reins of their animals as the other three men moved forward.

Risley and Grumpy walked to where Old Brindle lay on his side. The steer's head was turned so the horns pointed from the ground to the sky. A red-black hole showed where the steer's right eye had been. Only a step or two away, Ramey lay on his back. The gun was still in his hand.

MEETING PEOPLE

"Boss?" Whitsup stood over one of the coyotes. The two older men crossed the torn ground to join him. Whitsup lifted the coyote's head with the toe of his boot. "What do you think?"

Risley bent for a closer look then stood up and cleared his throat. His lips tightened into a thin line. He looked at Grumpy.

The old cowboy took off his hat and again wiped his face with his shirt sleeve. He stared into the inside of his hat. "Did you see his arm?"

Risley nodded.

Whitsup looked from one to the other. "Ramey's arm? Are you saying these two coyotes ripped him up and killed him?"

"No, I'm not" Grumpy's head snapped up. "He killed himself after killing Old Brindle. But these coyotes? They made him do it."

Whitsup stared down at the smaller coyote's open mouth. The jagged teeth and dried blood still looked bad. A shiver ran down his back. "They had rabies and gave it to—"

"Yes," Risley spoke up. He wiped a hand across his eyes then looked around at the faces of his upset cowboys. "We don't want other wild things getting at them and spreading it. We have a whole lot of digging to do. We have to bury these animals and--"

"The boy," Grumpy said for him.

"No, not a boy. It took a man to decide what he did. We are burying a man."

--The End --

Notes about the events of this story: This story is based on real events that happened to cowboys in the Old West. The events were written about in diaries.

After the Civil War, the people of Texas didn't have much money. Not enough men came back from the war to do the needed work. But, there were a lot of cattle running wild. They had to be rounded up and put into herds to be sold. Boys took men's jobs to make a living as cowboys. These cowboys helped drive the big herds of cattle from Texas to the railroads in Kansas. The days were long and the work hard. Sometimes that work cut short their lives

MEETING PEOPLE

DUMB ANIMALS DON'T THINK
GLOSSARY

barrels – round wooden kegs for storing things.

bellow – a sound louder than normal coming from an animal or a person.

brand – a way a person marks an animal to show who owns it.

brindle – color markings on an animal; dark stripes across the back of a dark animal.

British – a person or thing from Great Britain or England.

brush – an area with lots of trees and bushes.

buckskin – a tan colored horse with dark mane and tail, a dark line down its back from mane to tail, and dark legs.

canyon – an area of land surrounded by high rocks, mountains, or hills; sometimes narrow, sometimes wide, made by a stream or rain runoff eating away at the soil over a long time.

cinch – the leather strap around the horse's belly that holds a saddle on a horse's back.

corral – a pen for holding horses or cattle.

cough – a clearing of the throat or lungs.

cowboy – someone who works with cattle and horses on a ranch.

diary – a book where a person writes down thoughts or notes about each day. Plural is diaries.

excitement – showing great happiness or interest.

forehead – the top part of a person's face between the hair line and the eyes.

foreman – boss man who gives orders and plans the work the rancher wants done.

grab – take hold with a hand.

graze – eating grass, as herd animals do.

gritted -- jaws or teeth tight as if in pain or anger.

gully – a narrow opening in the ground made by running water.

lightning – flashes and streaks of white light in the sky during a storm.

loop – a circle, such as a circle made with the end of a rope used to catch an animal.

milling – many animals or people moving around.

point (riding point) – to ride at or near the front of a herd of animals to lead them in the line of travel.

MEETING PEOPLE

rabies – a deadly disease spread by animal bites; the word "mad" sometimes refers to an animal with rabies who drools, falls down, does not act right, and attacks anything in its path.

rancher – a person who owns enough land to raise cattle, horses, or sheep.

saddle – a seat for a person to sit atop a horse with stirrups for the person's feet, usually made of leather and held on the horse by a cinch that goes around its belly.

saddlebags -- cloth or leather sacks or bags that are tied behind the saddle and hang down each side of the horse to contain the rider's things.

Senor – a Spanish word for "Mister."

sleeve – the part of a shirt or coat covering the arm.

spur – a piece of metal worn on a boot heel and held in place by a leather strap around a cowboy's boot, used to touch the horse's sides to make him go faster. Called spurs in paired set.

stampede – when a herd or group of cattle or horses get scared and suddenly run.

steer – a male member of a cattle herd not used for breeding.

stirrup – the part of the saddle where the riders puts a foot.

tense – nervous or worried with muscles tight.

trot – a choppy way to move faster than a walk but slower than a run.

wrangler – the person who takes care of the horses on a ranch or a cattle drive.

yeah – a way of saying "yes."

MEETING PEOPLE

DUMB ANIMALS DON'T THINK
MENTOR QUESTIONS

Q1. Why do you think Ramey left home?

Q2. What kind of a boy do you think Ramey was at the beginning of the story? Give examples.

Q3. What did Ramey think of animals at the beginning of the story? How was that different from the way his father seemed to think about animals?

Q4. Why did Ramey make an X when the rancher told him to sign his name in the record book?

Q5. How do you think Ramey and the horse wrangler felt about each other? Why might they have felt that way?

Q7. What happened at the river?

Q8. What did Ramey find in the canyon?

Q9. What did Ramey do in the canyon and why?

Q10. Why did Risley call Ramey a man for doing such a horrible thing as kill himself?

DUMB ANIMALS DON'T THINK
POSSIBLE ANSWERS

A1. Answers may vary: Ramey needed the money. He wanted to get away from home or his mom. He wanted to be a real cowboy.

A2. He was not very nice and not very dependable. He left his mom alone, telling her she could do the work. He took the only horse. He kicked at the dog and didn't care that what happened to it. He left the gate open. He didn't respect animals.

A3. Ramey thought the only value animals had was to be used. He didn't respect them. He didn't think animals could think or have feelings. The trail boss said Ramey's dad respected animals and treated them well.

A4. Ramey probably could not read or write.

A5. The cowboys thought Old Brindle was smart, mean, and dangerous. Some of them thought the steer was the real boss of the cattle and maybe of the men. Some of the cowboys seemed to think the steer was as smart as the men.

A6. The two boys did not respect each other. They did not seem to like each other. They almost fought. Reasons may vary, but may include any of the following: Maybe they didn't like each other because they were close to the same age and possible rivals. Ramey may not have liked the Mexican boy for being better educated, more respectful and caring of the horses, and he had a well-regarded role on the cattle drive. Perhaps Ramey was prejudiced, jealous of the wrangler's confidence, and might have thought a wrangler was not as important the role as a cowboy.

A7. Several answers might work: Ramey switched his buckskin for a strong swimming horse. Ramey knew he would be forced to cross the dangerous river because it was his job to drive the cattle across. He thought taking only Old Brindle across before all the other cattle would be less risky. Ramey couldn't secure his rope and hold Old Brindle. The steer pulled Ramey and Whitsup into the river. An uprooted tree rammed into Ramey and scared his horse. A big wave rolled Ramey off his horse. He went over Old Brindle but was able to hang onto one horn and his cowhide. The steer carried him to shore. He rolled away then ran for a tree, but Old Brindle didn't chase him. Whitsup chased off the tired and watching steer.

A8. Ramey followed Old Brindle's tracks into the canyon. He found the steer being attacked by the two sick coyotes. His scared horse bucked him off just when he was getting his gun out of his saddlebags. One of the coyotes attacked him as he was trying to get up.

A9. Ramey shot the coyote that bit him then shot the coyote attacking Old Brindle. He talked to the steer as if he finally saw the animal could think and understand why he had to kill him. Then he immediately shot himself.

A10. The entire story Ramey had acted like a rude, know-it-all young boy. Risley saw that in the end Ramey had taken responsibility for not letting Old Brindle or himself suffer or spread the disease to others. That was the action of a mature man, not a selfish boy. At that time rabies had no cure.

TORY RUNNING

A MYSTERY

Tory ran alone. It proved how little she cared. Dressed in shorts, tube top, and no shoes, she ran beside the lake. Her feet hurt. It didn't matter. She wanted that pain to take away the hurt in her heart.

Gulping the stale air, she ran on. Her sorrow hurt more than her feet hitting the path. She stared up at the black sky and the dots of stars.

"Alone . . . alone," she said to herself.

How many times had Uncle T.J. told her not to run like this? "There are too many crazy people in the world. I'll never let you run alone, young lady. Never alone. Remember that."

People didn't scare her any more. Not like they did. Not like when he first took her in—after her parents died. At that time she did fear being alone. Her uncle knew that. He used it against her. He also used it for her. Now it was too late to tell him how much she understood his love. With a groan, Tory ran harder.

Uncle T.J. would say one word. Or he would look at her with his sweet smile. That was all it took to make her think. His peace of mind had helped her lost soul that first year—that bad year.

At first she had said no to all his offers. Those offers were for college, clothes, his friendship, all the things young girls needed. He waited for her to heal. He had no children. He had never married. How had he known what to do?

He was a writer. In fact, he had been a very good writer. He made up stories about why people did things. Was that why he understood her, too? Maybe it was because she was too much like him.

When she cried, he sat beside her. He waited in silence. Tory learned to accept things. When she yelled, he shrugged. She learned patience. When she trashed his home, he cleaned up after her. Actually, he was always cleaning. The day she joined him in doing the housework, he teased her. She had laughed with him then.

But sleep was another matter. Tory still couldn't sleep. He couldn't help her with that. So the writer had changed how he lived to be with her. He slept in the daytime and wrote in the late hours of the night. Then he asked her to jog with him around the lake. Why had he done that? He knew her body would get tired enough for her mind to sleep, too. What a wise man he had been.

Slowly he had stirred her to learn, to live. Now he was dead.

"Here I am . . . alone . . . again."

Tory slipped and almost fell. Stopping, she bent over. She put her hands on her bare knees. The sobs shook her body. A breeze of damp night air lifted her hair. It chilled her heated face.

"Never alone," a voice said.

Tory stood up fast. Her breath came in puffs. She listened harder. She tried to see into the night around her. Then she stared at the black lake. Someone, something was near, watching her.

Far away an owl hooted. Frogs croaked at one another. A little animal moved through the tall grass. A fish flopped out in the lake. The water lapped against the mud shore. Had her mind heard that sound as words? Was she "the crazy one" here? And who cared?

Tory jogged on at her easy pace. Her feet hit the path, but she didn't feel it now. She listened only to the sound of the lake's slap and swish, slap and swish . . . .

"9-1-1, Sheriff's Department," the operator said. No answer. "Hello! Can I help you?" The woman listened hard, trying to hear any sound. She heard a soft groan. It almost sounded like a cat mewing. Then she heard a thud. Was someone fighting? Were they hurt? Were they tied up?

She touched the caller I.D. button. It read "T.J. Fletcher." Within minutes she had the deputy on his way. He was driving to one of two new houses at Lake Connolly. It wouldn't take Jack Connolly long to get to the address. He had been raised on the farm next to the lake. He liked to drive around the area when he could. Jack knew every inch of the new streets.

MEETING PEOPLE

Jack turned off his lights at the corner. He drove in the middle of the empty street.

The street lights were not working yet. Jack was glad. It was one less man-made sign on the peaceful land. No one else in the Sheriff's Department shared his feelings. A well-lit housing area was less likely to have crime. Up until now, the only 9-1-1 call from the area had come in a week ago. T.J. Fletcher had a heart attack while swimming in the lake.

A shiver spread across Jack's broad back. He remembered how he had not been able to help. His wet clothes had stuck to his body that day. His shoulders and back had hurt as he carried Fletcher to the shore. His hands had pushed down on the man's cold, wet chest. Jack's lungs and warm lips had forced air into the man's cold, purple mouth.

Jack remembered a young woman. She had screamed at his side. He hadn't paid her much attention. All his efforts were on making the man's chest work. He hadn't helped.

A stronger shiver ran across Jack's body. His leg stiffened. His foot hit the brake. He leaned out the open window to take a deep breath. His mind cleared with the smell of the lake. He forgot the hum of the car's motor as he drove on. The friendly night sounds relaxed and calmed him. A quarter of a mile ahead, the street curved. Soft light shone through the patio doors of the Fletcher house.

A tall shadow moved on the far side of the patio. Jack lifted his foot off the gas and put his hand on his gun. As the car rolled to a stop, he opened the door. His left hand took up the flashlight. He held the gun in his right. Making no sound, he slid from the car and ran across the long, wet grass.

His eyes had not left the shadow. He stopped at the patio corner. The shadow was gone. Jack found nothing. Not a bush or flower pot or lawn chair. He looked around the bare patio. The open yard spread to the lake's edge.

Jack turned on his big flashlight and swept the area. He started to turn off the light, but something made him stop. He bent down for a better look. Small, bloody footprints. And larger, muddy shoe prints. Both sets of prints crossed the patio to the open door.

The deputy set down the flashlight. He used both hands to steady the gun. Then he used it to move aside the curtain. His gaze swept across the tidy room. A blonde women in shorts and a tight top slept on the couch. He glanced down at the floor. The bloody prints tracked into the room. The shoe prints stopped at the doorway.

The sleeping woman let out a cry. Her arms and nice legs beat at the soft cushions.

Jack stepped in and to the side. His back pressed against a bookcase. He was beside the fireplace. With his gun ready, he waited. No one else showed up. The woman curled into a ball. She cried softly but was still asleep.

MEETING PEOPLE

The telephone sat on the breakfast bar between the kitchen and the family room. The phone lay on its side beside its power station. Jack decided the pretty young woman was alone. He walked to the bar as he put his gun away. He picked up the mobile unit.

"Phyllis?" he said softly.

"What's going on, Jack? Do you need help?"

"I don't think so. Have you heard anything else since you called me?

"No, just the cries. What did you find?"

"A woman by herself, asleep but upset. I think she laid the phone down and accidently hit the emergency dial. She probably just wants company. I'll be 10-7 for about fifteen or twenty minutes." He hung up. The code 10-7 meant he would be out of his car at the scene.

Jack thought his time was being wasted. "Just another crazy person," he said to himself. Too bad she had to be so pretty, too. He stepped back to the patio doorway before he called out to the young woman.

"Ma'am!" He raised his voice. "Ma'am!"

Her thick eyelashes fluttered. She sat up, staring at him with wide, cat-green eyes. Once the redness and puffiness went away, those eyes would be beautiful, he thought.

"Who are you?" she demanded.

"County Deputy Jack Connolly, ma'am. Sorry I startled you, but I came to a 9-1-1 call from this address."

Her hand rubbed her forehead. She stared past him and shook her head. "I didn't call. I turned off the phone yesterday. I didn't want to hear another person say they were sorry."

"Maybe you dialed in your sleep?"

"Sleep? I never sleep at night. I haven't for four years now, not since my parents died." Her voice faded.

"Ma'am, you were asleep when I stepped through this patio door."

Anger sparked in her eyes. So did disbelief. "I couldn't have been. You're wrong. I don't sleep at night! And . . . not at all since . . . my uncle's funeral."

"Three days is a long time to go without sleep."

"How did you know it was three days?"

Jack looked away. He moved from one foot to the other. He didn't want this to become personal.

Her mouth dropped open. She pointed a shaky finger. "I remember. You're the one . . . who tried to save him."

"Yes, ma'am. I'm sorry I wasn't able to do that."

"No, it wasn't your fault. You seemed so big and strong. I thought you could do it, but I saw that no one could." Her voice softened. Tears came to her eyes. "Uncle T.J. didn't try to live. He was ready to go, ready to leave me alone. I was the one who wasn't ready." She shrugged.

"Ah, you seem to be bleeding, ma'am. Your feet."

"Tory Fletcher. Call me Tory, not ma'am." She stood up, looking more tired than in pain. "My feet? They don't hurt. Not at all." She walked toward the kitchen. "See? I'm fine."

Of course she was fine. She probably just put on this act. Maybe just to get someone out here. She wanted someone to feel sorry for her. Or did she?

Jack moved to leave. Then he remembered the two sets of prints. They had crossed the patio. Maybe someone had come by, someone she didn't know.

"How did you hurt your feet?" he asked.

The young woman looked around the kitchen. She seemed to be seeing it for the first time. "I ran around the lake, barefoot." She flipped the kitchen light switch. He face looked surprised. "I run every night between three and four."

Her frown deepened as she slowly turned in a full circle. As if in fear, she opened one cabinet door. Then she opened another and another.

"What's going on?"

"Ma'am?"

She turned those cat eyes on him. Her voice had been so soft before that her sharp words surprised him. "My uncle was very neat and clean. I wasn't. I kind of . . . trashed the place. I left dirty dishes. I broke up his plants. The garbage had spilled over there. I even tore up pillows and left that foam everywhere." She clenched her hands together. "Now, it's all cleaned up. Everything's put away, and I . . . I didn't do it."

Jack sighed. She had to be crazy. Either that or she was trying to keep him there.

"Calm down," he said. "You don't remember sleeping. Maybe you don't remember cleaning."

Tory shook her head. "No, I wasn't ready to do that, not yet. No! Someone was here." She hugged herself. Then she headed down the dark hallway. "And they opened the door to Uncle T.J.'s office. He never left it open." She turned on the office light and stood for a moment. "Everything is just as he left it." Her face looked confused again as she returned to the kitchen.

Jack was done playing the game. "I'm sure this is all because you aren't sleeping. The mind plays tricks when someone doesn't sleep. Things seem okay now. Just remember to close and lock all doors from now on. I need to get back on patrol."

He didn't wait for her say anymore. He stepped onto the patio. Then he bent to pick up his flashlight. It was gone. He knew he had set it down beside the doorway. Jack knelt to peer along his own path. The light through the patio door clearly showed a pair of footprints crossing the cement.

"What's the matter?" Tory asked from behind him.

Cold air whirled around him. He jumped to his feet and stared at the patio curtain. It had not moved in that strange wind he just felt. Pretty Tory stood in the doorway.

"I-I set down my flashlight out here. As I was looking for it . . . Well, here are your tracks."

"Tracks?"

He stepped aside and pointed. "Your feet left a bloody trail across the patio."

She frowned. "And those are your footprints?"

"No, I'm wearing boots. Those were made by some kind of track shoe. See the pattern?"

"Like running shoes?" Tory whispered.

He heard the fear in her voice. She backed away then turned toward the hallway.

Without a word, Jack followed. She opened another door in the darkness. When she flipped the light on, a mud room was revealed. It had washer, dryer, and cabinets on the right and coat hooks on the wall to the left. On a mat next to the back door sat two pair of running shoes, one pair small, the second large, both covered in dry mud.

She turned to see his reaction.

"What's your point, ma'am? The patio tracks are fresh mud and those are long dried."

"Uncle T.J. ran with me the night before . . . before . . . ."

Jack had worked a twelve hour shift that night. His memory was clear. "You ran in a rain storm?"

She nodded. "Like I said, I run every night, no matter what. Uncle T.J. once said the lake comforts me."

A smile tugged at his lips but the pain in her face stopped it. "My family owned this land. I know the lake. I do understand about its comfort." He cleared his throat. "My point is . . . these shoes didn't make the fresh tracks on your patio."

"No kidding!" Her cat's eyes looked angry again. "Deputy, I am not crazy, just upset. So, you think someone followed me tonight on my run . . . my barefoot run?"

Her up-and-down moods worried him. But, he could also see her inner strength rising. For some reason he wanted her to be strong and not afraid. He also wanted her to know he was there to help if really needed.

"It could be." He thought to try teasing her. "Even in the country, we have crazy people. The world is full of them, you know."

Tory's body jerked as if he had slapped her. Her eyes grew big with fear.

He realized his mistake too late and waved his hand. "Bad joke. I want you to know I'm here to take care of those kinds of people. Don't worry. If someone was around, I probably scared him off. I can check your doors and windows, if you want."

She licked her lips. "Only if you have time." With a shaky hand, she rubbed her forehead. "All I want or need is some coffee."

She combed her hair with her long fingers. Jack watched those hands. Her eyelids closed as she rolled her head to help a stiff neck. He wanted . . . or was it a needed . . . to touch her just once. He cleared his throat instead.

"I'd say you need sleep more than coffee."

The thick lashes lifted. "Uncle T.J. only drank tea. He teased me about my coffee." She blinked and snapped out of her deep thoughts. "After you leave I'm having coffee, shower, sleep, in that order, Deputy Jack Connolly. With or without your advice."

Jack blew out a long breath. He had just been put in his place. "Whatever you say, ma'am."

"Ma'am," she repeated. "I may be just an upset female asking . . . but are you always so polite? You hold people away . . . so you are in control?"

"I, ah . . . ." It was his turn to blink. He blushed.

"Exactly." She left him to his business.

He checked the back door and found it locked. He went up the dark hall into the two small bedrooms. Their window locks wouldn't move. At the open door to the master bedroom, Jack stopped. The bedroom was now an office. This doorway and the room felt different. He shivered.

"Sorry to bother you, Fletcher," he whispered. Now, why had he said that?

He spun the round switch to turn the light to full brightness. Jack nodded at what he saw. The room had been changed into a writer's special place. It had bookcases, a U-shaped desk, a computer, and a printer. A very old typewriter sat on the messy table below a big picture window. The man had probably enjoyed looking out at the lake as he worked.

"Wow, Fletcher," Jack said. "You must have put in extra heating and cooling vents to make up for the window. The air conditioning is keeping this room meat-market cold."

He recalled Tory's comment about the open door. He pulled it closed behind him.

With his rounds completed, Jack said a quick good-bye. He left the house to go back on patrol. Bits and pieces of the events played in his mind for the rest of his shift. Tory Fletcher was either sick with grief or a little crazy or a woman he would like to know better. It bothered him that he couldn't decide which.

In the morning light, Jack struggled to write his report. He typed out that Tory was "upset due to recent loss." He read his words again. They seemed right . . . yet wrong. He finally slapped the printout onto his boss's desk.

Nothing went right on his day off. Jack returned to work at the Sheriff's Department at seven the next night. He spoke only in single word answers. People around the office left him alone.

Then his boss's joke made him mad. Of course the boss said he didn't write the note, but Jack knew no one else had read his report. The man had to be the one to print out the two words left on the sheet of paper on Jack's desk. They read: TORY RUNNING.

Tory rolled the pencil between her fingers. She looked at the pencil. Her lip curled. Why did she have habits such as chewing on pencils and running in the middle of the night? School kids ate their pencils. She'd never heard of anyone else who ran at night. No one.

"No one in their right mind!" she whispered to herself.

She slammed the book closed on the pencil. Then she dropped the book on top of her blank notepad. She couldn't study anyway.

The Grandmother clock on the mantle bonged three times.

"Never alone," a voice whispered.

Tory shot out of the chair and spun around. "This is not funny! I am not laughing. And I'm not afraid. So there!"

Her heartbeat slowed. She took a deep breath, wet her lips, and waited. The silence closed around her.

"Stop it, Tory. Your mind is working too hard. You've showered, napped, and eaten as planned. You even cleaned your running shoes. How about a run so you can wear them? No more trail of blood for some cowboy-type deputy to find."

She remembered Deputy Connolly's blue eyes. His tan face, his size, his words came back to her thoughts.

He had almost said she was crazy. She had not cleaned the house . . . She had not been asleep. She told him that, and he hadn't believed her. Of course, he thought she was crazy. A blush heated her face. Why should she care what some deputy thought of her? She knew what she had and hadn't done. She knew what she could and couldn't do.

"I'm going for a run like I always do!"

She stopped at her bedroom door and turned toward the office. The light was on. "I know I turned off that light. Don't tell me this new house has a short in the wiring. A good college student I may be, but a Fix-it Lady I am not!" She clicked the switch and the office lights went out . . . again.

Several minutes later, Tory closed the back door on the dark house. The lock jammed several times before it clicked.

"Is everything falling apart?" she demanded. She kicked the door just to make her point. Then she got ready to run.

Behind her house at the lake's edge, she moved her body to warm up. On her second jumping jack, a bright light shone on her. She brought up her hand to cover her eyes.

"Who's there?"

"Me again, Miss Fletcher," Jack Connolly called out.

"Point that thing somewhere else, will you?"

"Sorry, ma'am." The beam slanted to the ground. It lit his way toward her.

"Can I help you, Deputy? I didn't find your other flashlight. Is that what you are looking for?"

"No. I guess the question is 'Can I help you?'"

Tory planted her hands on her hips. "Are you trying to be funny?"

The tall man stopped about six feet from her. He switched off the light. They stepped closer to each other in the darkness. He seemed so big beside her. Tory shivered, despite the summer night and the warmth of her sweat suit.

"We got another 9-1-1 call from your number."

"No, you didn't, because I didn't make another one. I didn't make the first one, ah, Jack is it?"

"Caller I.D. doesn't make mistakes. At 3:05 a.m. the 9-1-1 operator taped a call from your house."

"And whose voice is on that tape?" She clenched her teeth to control her temper.

"No voice. Just the call. I want you to understand something, ma'am. We overlook certain things two times. I repeat, two. Another trick call means I'll have to write a ticket and there will be a fine."

The office light snapped on. It streamed through the picture window, shining directly on the couple.

"You have company?" Jack asked.

"No." She tripped as he jerked her to the side. "Just a minute, cowboy." Her hand brushed against the badge on his chest. She pushed herself away from his solid body. "I've been having trouble with that light switch all night. I think it's a short in the wiring."

"Okay, Miss Fletcher. Let's go check it out. I'll hang up your phone while we're at it."

Tory glared at him before she stomped ahead of him. Remembering the bad lock, she pushed in the key and turned it hard. She opened the door and swept her hand for him to enter. "After you, Jack."

The deputy unsnapped his gun. Just as he stepped inside, Tory flipped on the mud room's light. His jaw clenched in anger, but he ignored her. Slowly, he opened the hallway door. He moved toward the office.

"Oh, for crying out loud!" Tory said. She pushed past him and entered the room. "See? No one is hiding here. It's just a dead man's office. And the electricity has gone crazy, not me!"

Jack dropped his new flashlight through its belt loop. "That's a snippy way to act after what happened a couple of days ago, Tory."

"You know where the phone is."

She kept her back to him. She stared at her image in the black of the picture window. Tears blurred the image. It moved and grew larger, much larger. Someone had stepped up behind her. A warm hand gently pressed between her shoulder blades.

"Don't touch me! I don't need your . . ." She looked over her shoulder, expecting to see Jack Connolly. " . . . pity," she finished. No one was there. She tried to draw a breath, but couldn't. The faint hand patted and moved across her stiff back.

Footsteps sounded in the hallway. Then Connolly stood in the doorway. "The phone was on and the 9-1-1 operator was on the other end. What do you say to that?"

Tory finally gasped a short breath then another and another. The deputy frowned. Tory knew she was breathing too fast. She couldn't stop to answer him. Jack's face changed from anger to worry. He stepped closer. The warmth around her faded. His hands grabbed her shoulders.

"Whoa there. You look about to faint. It's really cold in this room, so you can't have a summer heat stroke. Take one deep, deep breath. Now another breath." He helped her out to the family room and to a seat on the couch. "I'll close the back door. Then I'll get you a glass of water."

Tory tried to blank all the thoughts from her mind. The pictures came back anyway. She saw herself running beside her uncle. The pictures melted as Connolly's footsteps returned. When he didn't speak, she opened her eyes. He stood beside her, looking down at a long silver flashlight he held in his hands. Water dripped from it.

"What?" she asked.

"This is my old flashlight. It's the one I set down the other night out on your patio. Here are my initials. I found it just now . . . in the middle of the back doorway."

"Why is it all wet?"

"I don't know. How did we miss it coming in that door? Unless . . . we . . . didn't. Unless someone set it there just now."

"Right! Someone is playing a sick joke. And I don't think you're funny!"

His head came up. "Me? You're the one faking the calls and this fainting act. I don't have time for this! I'm out of here. Don't call me; I'll call you!"

Jack tried to slam the back door. It wouldn't catch. He set down the wet flashlight and pulled out his new one. Its glow instantly showed the door and the problem. Someone had scratched the latch and the lock below it. That someone had bent the metal and marked up the wood.

"You are one strong, but quiet bad guy," he whispered to himself.

Jack put the new flashlight back on his belt. He walked slowly back to his car. Someone was out there hiding, waiting, watching. Someone had left the wet flashlight. Why? Maybe a calling card? Or a warning?

The area was dark. Jack tried to recall details of what he could not see. It was a new housing area with lots of building going on. The big yards had been cleared of trees and bushes. Each plot was shaped as a little hill. The house would be at the top. The yards gently sloped down to the lake. A few young trees had been left in the dips between the plots. Those dips were the property lines. The lake's shore had been cleared of brush. There were no hiding places. The Fletcher house had been built first. Just one other house had been finished. It was on the other side of the lake. Something didn't feel right.

"Feel right? Now Tory's got you thinking crazy thoughts, Connolly," he talked to himself. But the shoe prints, the marks on her lock, and the wet flashlight were real. Someone knew she was alone. "But where are you? And what kind of sick game are you playing?" he whispered.

His left hand grew cold from gripping the watery flashlight. Jack unlocked the car door and threw the thing into the other seat. He rubbed his hand on his leg to warm his fingers.

"Now I'm really going crazy!" he said as he slid into his seat. He reached for his clipboard. "So, who is the craziest, Jack? You, her, some stalker? Why not a ghost? Maybe Old T.J. himself? There's a thought for tonight's report." He threw the clipboard on top of the old flashlight then reached for the car's radio.

Jack called in that he was back in service. That was the easy part. Driving away from that house took more effort. Instead of driving around his usual streets, he turned off his headlights and made a U-turn at the top of the hill where his family home had once stood. He looked down at the single light in the house he had just left. When it went out, he shut off his car's engine and coasted back down to the street curve in front of the Fletcher house.

Tory ran a quarter of a mile along the lake. The wind blew a spray of water into her face. Startled, she stopped. The wind died down, yet the lake water still slapped against the shore. It sounded angry. Tory wiped the mist from her face. She pulled at her head band and got ready to run again.

Thick, wet arms grabbed her. They yanked her backwards against a fat body. Her arms were pinned to her sides. Her ribs almost gave way. Tory could only kick and gasp. The heels of her running shoes beat against his hard shins. When she forced a deep breath to scream, a big hand closed across her face. Her lungs burned. Finally, the thumb moved from over her nose and she drew in enough air to keep from fainting.

"Now, let's go home, pretty thing," a deep voice said in her ear. She was lifted. The man easily walked back along the path, holding her in front of him.

"I like a fighter, you know. Night after night, I watched those long legs of yours carry you around the lake. I could tell you were strong. Skinny but strong. You'll take a long time, but every minute will be worth it. I got mighty cold in that lake, but you'll warm me up, won't you?"

This isn't happening. This isn't happening. Her thoughts said the same words over and over.

She fought. Her sweat suit soaked up the water from the man's clothes. She grew cold and wet. Fishy lake water, mud, and sour body smells choked her. Acid bubbled up in her throat. She stiffened.

"Oh, baby, you are going to be fun. I thought that police boy would never leave us alone."

Her thoughts raced. Alone. Never alone. You warned me, Uncle T.J.

Crushed and helpless, Tory shook. Wave after way of shivers hit her. The fat man almost had her home.

Jack stared at the dark Fletcher house. Again he tried to make sense of the events that had brought him here in the first place. He rubbed his left hand on his leg.

"Man!" He shook the hand. "It still feels cold."

Not cold. Wet! He grabbed the old flashlight. Water leaked from it. The smell of musty lake water rose like a cloud to fill his nose and mouth. "The lake! He has to be in the lake!"

With gun in hand, he ran around the house. He reached Tory's back door. It stood open. Warnings rang in his mind. Taking one careful step at a time, Jack reached the hallway. Both bedroom doors were open. He quickly looked in each. Empty.

Where is Tory?

At the open office door, he stopped. Across the dark room, the picture window looked odd, flat like it was dirty or coated so it wouldn't show an image. It drew him forward. As he leaned across the desk, he put his left hand down for balance. It rested on the old typewriter. The biting cold of the metal shot up his arm. He pulled away. Then he looked closer. A sheet of paper had been rolled into place.

Jack started to pull out his new flashlight, but stopped. He realized the light might be seen. He pulled the paper out of the typewriter and hurried to the kitchen. His arm pushed dishes to the back of the counter. He laid down the paper. He bent over to block the light as he flicked on his flashlight. Its beam showed two words: TORY RUNNING.

Jack stood up. The same words left on his desk! Warm air blew across his cheek as if someone laughed next to his ear. The flashlight dropped from his fingers. Its long beam rolled back and forth across the counter. It showed the dishes he had shoved back. He stared at the tea pot and a steaming cup of tea. Not Tory's coffee, but T.J. Fletcher's tea. And the breath of warmth on his face had smelled of tea!

"This is crazy," he whispered. Holding the gun tighter he backed away.

The flashlight rolled off the counter. It thudded on the carpet and went out. The house was dark again.

A moaning cry at the back door put him on alert. The sounds of a struggle came from the mud room then the hallway. And he heard a man's voice.

"Oh, pretty thing, I like the night and a dark house, just like you do. I know all about you. I've been watching a long time. Let's get in here and finally get to the fun part."

Tory grabbed at thoughts. Here? Uncle T. J.'s house? Not here. No!

She went limp. The hand on her mouth slipped. Tory managed one weak cry. Then he almost crushed her face with his grip. She bent and bucked as he carried her across the mud room. As they moved into the hallway, she kicked the walls as much as she kicked him.

"That's the way, baby. Fight me good! Our first-time fun is going to be in the old man's office. In the dark, on the floor. I wish you were in those shorts and the rag top."

The man threw her onto her back on the office floor. It knocked the wind out of her. Her throat closed as his fat, wet knees pushed her legs apart. Her arms and hands tingled as blood returned to them. She squeezed her eyes shut.

"We'll pretend his ghost is sitting at that desk. He's typing a story. We are inspiring him."

Bright light flooded the room. Tory threw a numb arm across her eyes. Panic roared in her ears. White light and colors swirled in her mind.

"One more move and you'll inspire me to pull the trigger of this gun pressed to the back of your head."

Tory fell into blackness. It seemed like only a moment passed. The darkness faded to gray. The roaring in her ears changed to an echo.

"Never alone!"

Tory's eyes flew open. She pulled a wet cloth from her forehead to stare up into Jack Connolly's blue eyes. They were beautiful eyes, dark with worry. He truly worried about her? Her heart skipped a beat.

"What did you say?" she whispered.

"I was talking to the medics here. I said you were old enough to know better. You run, but should be never alone." He gently replaced the cloth and whispered the order, "Never alone."

Tory relaxed. She was safe now. A smile grew on her lips. "The three times rule."

"What?"

She smiled so hard her cheeks hurt. "I think that was the third time I heard those words. Uncle T.J. said writers have to make a point three times for readers to get it." She again lifted the cloth.

Jack's lips fought a smile. "So what's your point?"

"For me the point is good-bye."

He blinked. "Good-bye to what?"

"Tory running . . . alone. Uncle T.J. said I should always have a running partner. I got his message."

Jack looked at the typewriter by the window. "I think I did, too." He allowed a full smile this time. "When did you say you like to run?"

--The End--

TORY RUNNING
GLOSSARY

advice – words given to help people.

air conditioning – units to cool the air in a house or business in the heat of summer.

attention – looking at, listening to, speaking to someone or something.

believe – to think something is true.

blink – to quickly close and open the eyes.

blonde – pale yellow to gold colored hair or someone having that color hair.

blush – face turning red due to uneasy feeling.

bonged – the sound big clocks make on the hour.

breeze – a light wind.

clench – close tightly such as to bite down or to close the hand to make a fist.

clipboard – a small board with a clip at the top to hold papers in place.

college – schools of higher learning beyond high school.

counter – top of a table or cabinet.

MEETING PEOPLE

crush – a hard squeeze or pressing down to stop in place.

deputy – a country sheriff's helpers

emergency dial – a phone button that quickly calls 9-1-1 for help.

faint – a person passes out; can be caused by little air, blood loss, shock, fear.

funeral – people coming together to talk about the person who died and help those left behind.

glare – a harsh stare when someone is angry or doesn't like something.

grab – to take and hold by force.

initials – the first letter of each of a person's names.

inspiring – to cause another person's actions or words.

jammed – the parts of a something are stuck and will not work the way they should.

Ma'am – short for "madam," a term of respect for a lady.

mobile unit – a phone that can be carried around.

mumble – to say quietly and not clearly.

mutter – to say quietly and not clearly.

operator – the person on a phone or radio who takes or directs calls medics – people who give first aide on the scene where people are hurt.

patience – to wait calmly

patio – an area for activities outside a house with a brick, cement, or wood floor.

protect – guard from bad things or people or save people from being hurt.

reaction – action, look on the face or in the eyes to something.

shin – front, hard part of the lower leg.

short – a bad part of wiring stopping the flow of electricity.

shrug – lifting of the shoulders to show something doesn't matter.

stalker – a bad person who watches and follows another person to hurt them.

startle – to surprise a person or an animal making them afraid.

sweat suit – shirt and pants worn while working out or running to soak up sweat.

whoa – another way to say "stop."

MEETING PEOPLE

TORY RUNNING
MENTOR QUESTIONS

Q1. What did Uncle T.J. warn Tory about? What do you think was his concern?

Q2. Why were Tory's feet bloody and why didn't she care?

Q3. Why was Jack sent to the Fletcher house the first time and what did he think? Who do you think made the 9-1-1 call and why?

Q4. Why did Jack come back to the Fletcher house? Why does Tory challenge him instead of welcoming him?

Q5. Why did Jack know the area so well? How did that help him solve this mystery?

Q6. What really upset Tory when she looked around the house while Jack was there?

Q7. Where had the man been hiding? And who had been giving clues about that?

Q8. What were some of the clues Jack found that made him think Tory was in danger?

Q9. What was the "Times Three Rule" and how did it apply to this story for Tory and for Jack?

Q10. Do you think Tory will run alone again? Why or why not?

TORY RUNNING
POSSIBLE ANSWERS

A1. He had warned to never run alone. The house was in a kind of isolated area and he knew a woman alone would be a target for "the crazy people of the world."

A2. She ran barefoot on the path around the lake, running so hard the skin on her feet broke. Her heart was hurting so much over her uncle's recent death that physical pain meant nothing to her. She was not sleeping and not acting or thinking normally.

A3. A 9-1-1 call came in but no one answered the operator so she worried the person on the other end was hurt or in danger. Police are always sent to check on such calls and Jack was the Deputy covering that area. When Tory denied making the call, Jack thought she was trying to get attention or she was so upset that she didn't remember doing it or she pressed the emergency dial on accident. Possibly the ghost of the recently dead T.J. Fletcher was reaching out for real help for his grieving niece who did not realize she was in danger.

A4. Jack is aware of his attraction to "Pretty Tory" but when the 9-1-1 Center gets a second call she denies, he has to warn her she could be fined. Tory has eaten and slept so she is starting to cope and is insulted that Jack refuses to believe her.

A5. Jack's farming family had owned the land and the lake is still named after them. He understands Tory's idea that the lake comforts her. Being close to that land, he is able to identify when "something is not right" and opens his reasoning to consider even bizarre possibilities. Possibly, because he couldn't save the uncle, he feels a little responsible for the vulnerable niece.

MEETING PEOPLE

A6. Tory vividly remembered how her uncle took care of her and the house when he was alive. So when she acted out the same way to his death as she had to her parents' passing, she cannot accept that she cleaned up her own grief-stricken messes, but she can't explain it either. In emotional turmoil, she resents Jack trying to provide logical explanations from a judgmental and controlling distance.

A7. The stalker had been submerging in the lake to watch Tory running. He had been spying on the Fletchers even before T.J. died. It is possible that after he died, T.J. saw the stalker and knew he was going to strike soon. T.J's first connection with Jack happened when Jack attempted to save him from drowning but couldn't save him from the heart attack. T.J. may have identified the exact protector Tory needed and does what he can to keep Jack coming back (with the 9-1-1 calls and taking the flashlight to the lake) until he can save Tory.

A8. The big muddy shoe prints coming to the open patio door put him on alert that someone had followed her. His flashlight went missing then it was returned after obviously being in the lake. A determined person had been working on the back door lock, trying to break in. He could not find a logical source of the TORY RUNNING attention-getting messages on his desk at the Sheriff's Department and on T.J.'s office typewriter. Tory told him she only liked coffee while T.J. only drank tea and he found freshly made steaming tea the night he decided to watch the house.

A9. Writers use a storytelling device to foreshadow something important by mentioning it three times. Tory had heard a mysterious voice saying "Never alone" three times then Jack emphasized it in the end. Jack had come back three times to check on and eventually rescue Tory, had gotten the TORY RUNNING messages twice then Tory opens herself to his help when she mentions it the third time. He gets the point.

TORY RUNNING

A10. Probably not. Jack asked what time Tory liked to run. It sounds like he is going to start running with her. She may have learned the lesson on why she shouldn't run alone.

THE GARDNER
A ROMANCE

Janet moved the curtain. A tall, thin man stood at the gate. His clothes looked ragged and dusty.

"Oh, no, not another bum," she whispered. Her fingers poked at the brown hair sliding from the bun at her neck.

A lot of men had lost their jobs in 1932. Some of them rode the empty rail cars to other parts of the country. Some just walked from town to town.

Before her father died, he had warned her, "Never talk to a bum. And don't feed one. That's like feeding a stray dog. He will keep coming back. You never know if he might hurt you or steal from you."

The man opened the gate. He walked slowly toward her front door.

Janet took a deep breath. She had to make the bum go away.

Before he could knock, she opened the door. He blinked his gray eyes in surprise. His big hand pulled his hat off. At least he had good manners.

"Howdy, Miss," he said in a soft voice.

Janet's chin lifted as he looked her up and down. Words would not form in her mind.

"Never met a woman as tall as I am," he said.

She started to close the door. He put his empty hand against it.

"I didn't mean anything bad by that. I . . . I . . ." He looked over his shoulder at her yard. "I saw a garden needing planting. I'm willing to work on your yard, too. I just need a meal. I would eat it here on the steps."

His shoulders were broad and manly. The gray eyes twinkled.

She looked him over. She liked what she saw and licked her lips. "That . . . garden needs more than one day's work. It always took my father a long time."

"How about just the yard work? Unless you don't have the extra food."

"I have enough. I just don't want your kind here." Her hand flew to her mouth. She couldn't believe she had been so rude. But she was alone. She couldn't let her guard down.

"My kind? Oh, you mean with no home, no money, wearing dirty clothes. I had a fine farm. The dust blew it away. I spent the last of my money burying my mom and dad. I wash when I can. I haven't been able to do that lately. Sorry to have bothered you."

He stared down at his feet. Wavy black hair fell onto his forehead. She couldn't see his eyes with his head bent. Janet knew they would not look angry. They would be sad, like his voice. She chewed her lip as he walked back toward her gate.

MEETING PEOPLE

An hour later, Janet tried to ram the shovel into the hard dirt. There had been very little rain in two years. The dirt was rock hard. For those two years her father had been too sick to do this. He had never taught her how to care for a garden. That was his job after the bank closed. She didn't even know how to plant one. But she had enough common sense to know the dirt had to be dug up.

She stabbed the dirt again. Her hands hurt and she had just started! This was taking so long, the spring season would be over before she even had the ground ready. Not one seed would get planted. She remembered her father carrying bucket after bucket of water from the well pump to wet the turned soil. Her shoulders ached.

"You aren't digging deep enough," a soft voice spoke from the fence.

Janet froze. Her eyes looked up. "Oh, it's you."

The man nodded. "You may be tall and strong, but I don't think you've ever done this before."

"No. I just canned and cooked what my father grew." The man waited, so she added, "He was sick then he died."

Once again the man took off his hat. He waved it at the big space beside the house. "Putting in a garden would take me a couple of weeks . . . if you have the seeds and such."

Janet's heart pounded in her chest. She had not wanted help from anybody since her father died. She didn't like pity. This could be different if she paid him. The cookie jar money was almost gone. How would she pay him? The important money had been hidden

THE GARDNER

away. She had just enough to get her through these hard times. There was no extra for a hired hand.

"Yes, I have the seeds and the potato starts to plant. What I don't have is money."

He shrugged. "Like I said before, just put a plate of food in my hand."

Now she could hardly draw a breath. "I have no place for you to stay . . . or to wash up."

His big smile made her a little dizzy. "I have a place to stay and wash up."

Janet remembered the hobo camp down by the river. The railroad bridge made noise when a train was near. Those who wanted to leave the camp had time to run up the bank. They jumped on the train as it slowed. Her father had told of seeing one man fall. The train ran over him. The town had to pay to bury what was left. Janet shivered.

"My father said my cooking was county fair good." She chewed her lip. Did he think that was bragging?

"Then I'll be paid well."

She finally smiled back at him. "And who will I be paying?"

"My name is Mike Wills, Miss Turner."

A tiny fear nibbled at her mind. She frowned. "How did you know my name?"

"I asked in town."

"Oh."

"Or do you like to be called Janet?"

She dropped the shovel. "Miss Turner will be just fine. I will leave you to your work. I will return to my house."

"A fine house like this needs a lot of tending."

"Yes, it does, Mr. Wills."

"Beans and ham."

"Pardon me?"

"The store clerk said you also make the best beans and ham in the county."

Janet quickly turned away. She didn't want him to see her blush.

At noon she set a plate of food and a glass of cool tea on the bench beside the back door. She covered the plate and glass with an open napkin. A warm breeze touched her face. She hoped the wind wouldn't blow any harder. Everything was so dry already.

One hand shaded her eyes so she could see the man. He had taken off his shirt. Sweat made his back shiny in the midday sun. Again, she had to bite her lip.

Her voice cracked as she called out, "Mr. Wills!"

As he turned, his arm wiped across his brow. The muscles in his chest rippled. How could a thin man have such muscles?

"I . . . I have food for you," she shouted a little too loudly.

She watched him walk to the fence and pick up his shirt. As he stepped through the gate, Janet pointed to the covered plate. Before he reached the back porch, she returned to the kitchen doorway.

He uncovered the plate. "Fried potatoes and onions. Canned peaches. Looks real good, Miss Janet," he said from outside of the screen door.

THE GARDNER

"The beans and ham will be supper tomorrow. They have to cook a long time." She thought he chuckled. "I prefer you call me Miss Turner, sir."

"But Miss Janet sounds better. Don't want to waste a pretty name." The bench creaked as he sat on it.

She drew a deep breath and shook her head. At the kitchen table she patted the pie dough into a ball. She didn't say anything back.

The next morning Mike Wills came at dawn to work the ground. Janet set out a saucer of milk on the porch step. She called for her kitty. Her gardener waved at her.

She pulled her robed closer around her small waist. Most days she made breakfast then dressed. That day she decided to dress first. She even heated a flat iron and pressed an apron. It had ruffles.

Wills came to the back door at her call. She invited him in to the table. He looked at the apron ruffles and smiled. Her insides warmed. She sat across from him, trying not to look up.

A large bite of pancakes disappeared into his mouth. His eyes closed. His pleased groan made her shiver. She told herself she was happy because she was cooking for someone else now. It wasn't because she liked pleasing this man.

Two days passed. Janet fixed breakfast, a noon meal, and supper for her hired man. He explained how to plant the different things and how much to plant. She even helped with the two long rows of potatoes. She worked side by side with him.

"So why didn't your father teach you all this?"

"He worked the garden as long as I can remember. He had an important job, but he loved this. He said the feel of the good earth made his heart full."

"What did he do in the winter?"

"Planned for the spring and summer."

They laughed together. When she frowned he sat back on his heels. He said, "I understand that. When he got sick, it must have bothered him not to be able to do this."

"Father was a proud man. A garden was his main way of providing for me with his own hands."

Wills nodded. His dirty hand waved at the house. "I heard he was the town banker. Everybody liked him. How was he able to keep the house when the bank went out of business?"

Janet stopped digging. "It was my mother's house. She left it to me in her will."

"And who pays the taxes?"

She didn't like the question. Hired hands didn't pry into other people's business. She stood. Brushing at her skirt just caused more smears. "I don't think that is any of your business, Mr. Wills."

His hand caught one of hers. She stood still. Then she looked into his eyes. Heat shot up her arm and straight into her chest.

"I'm sorry. I had to sell my farm to pay the taxes. It would be a shame if that happened to you."

"It won't."

"Good. That's good," he murmured and let go of her hand.

That night Janet tossed and turned in bed. Her father's warning about bums scared her. Was Mike Wills here to find her money? That thought bothered her. Why? She wanted to trust him. She wanted him to laugh and hold her hand. He didn't seem to think she was too tall or ugly. And he worked hard. Was her cooking enough to pay Mike? She fell asleep saying his first name.

The next morning Mike didn't come with the morning sun. Janet shrugged. She sat down to breakfast alone.

Minutes later a loud knock sounded. She looked up to see two men at her back door. One was heavy. The other was short. More bums. She glanced at the screen door. It was hooked.

"What do you want?"

"We were walking by and smelled those pancakes. Do you have any extra?" the big man asked. He didn't bother taking off his hat.

The short man pushed him aside. His hat stayed on his head, too. "Pay no mind to Frank, Miss. We've been on the road a long time. Are the train tracks close?"

"Yes. Follow the road out front. Go west. You'll find the tracks."

"Thanks. West? Do you know when the next train might come?"

She crossed her arms. The heavy man stared at her. She didn't like something about him. "No. I don't pay any attention."

The man named Frank pointed. "One place at the table. Are you eating all those pancakes piled on that platter?"

"There aren't that many. I have no extra batter to make more."

"So you won't be cooking for your man?"

Janet swallowed hard. If she admitted it, these two would know she was alone. For some reason they must not know. "My--"

"Her man is late getting back home," Mike's voice interrupted.

She sighed in relief. The two men stepped away from the door. Mike walked up the porch steps. "I brought a few more potato starts, Janet. Pastor Reed asked me to pick them up for our garden."

She glanced at the cloth sack in his hand then at his face. He wasn't looking at her. He was looking at the two men. He stood differently, like his whole body was a tight spring ready to let go. His eyes looked like cold steel. He didn't like these men either.

"Well, Mike," she started talking too quickly. "I'll just fix you--"

"Not hungry. I've got work to get to, and so do you. I'm sure these men understand."

"Sure. Sure, mister," the short man said. He pulled his friend's arm.

Janet opened the screen door. She stepped to Mike's side to watch them leave.

They heard the heavy man say, "With a house like this, you know she had food."

"Well, he didn't want to share. Just shut up," the short man said.

Janet felt Mike's hand slip around hers. He gave it a squeeze. Without looking at her, he went down the steps and toward the garden.

Again that night, she tossed and turned. She couldn't stop her mind. It had really happened. Mike had called himself her man. He must have meant her hired man. But he had squeezed her hand. Didn't that mean he cared about her? He couldn't be after her hidden money. How could he even know about it? She fell asleep crying.

A sound awakened her. The bedroom window was open to let in the cooling night breeze. Janet lay still and listened very hard.

Thump! Thump!

She got out of bed and tip-toed to the window. No moon lit the night sky. The stars gave almost no light. Her back yard below the window was very dark.

Thump! Thump!

A small light moved next to the cellar door. The light dimmed. It was a lantern sitting on the ground. In its shadow a figure bent over a spot beside the door. Someone had discovered where her money was buried!

Janet forgot she only wore a thin nightgown. She ran down the stairs. Her hand opened the back door very quietly. The shovel stood by the door. She took it in both hands. Her bare feet made no sounds on the steps or in the grass. She slipped along the wall toward the cellar door, the lantern, and the figure.

Swinging with all her might, Janet smacked the man high on his back. The thief grunted. He fell face down into the hole he had dug.

"Oh, Mike!" she groaned. "Why did you do this?"

"No, why did *you* do this?" his voice spoke behind her.

She turned but couldn't see him in the dark. He stepped to her side. Her hand flew to her chest. She wanted to cry and scream at the same time.

"I-I thought it was you," she finally whispered.

"So I gathered."

"Who-who is that?" She pointed a shaky finger at the downed man.

"Pastor Reed."

She gasped. "What?"

"You heard me."

Wills bent to lift the minister from the hole. The hurt man groaned.

"Oh, goodness! Did-did I hurt him?"

Wills chuckled then laughed. "Of course you hurt him. But you didn't kill him. Like I said before, you are one strong lady."

"Oh, ouch," moaned Pastor Reed. "What happened? What hit me?"

"A shovel," Wills answered.

"Mike? Oh, Mike, did those bums come back?"

"No, Pastor. I ran them off. Miss Janet here swung that mean shovel."

She wanted to slap Wills. Instead, she said, "Pastor Reed, I am so very sorry."

"Apology accepted. I hit my head going into the hole. It hurts. Got any ice in your icebox?"

"The iceman came today. Let's get you to the kitchen."

Janet and Mike each took one of the minister's arms. They walked him slowly across the yard and up the porch steps. Finally they lowered him to a kitchen chair.

Mike lit the table lamp then filled a glass from the water bucket. Janet used an ice pick to break chips from the block of ice in the bottom of her icebox. She wrapped the ice in a dish towel. Mike took that from her. Janet frowned at him. He acted as if this was his house. She didn't like it.

The injured man sipped some water then pressed the towel-wrapped ice to his head. "I'm the one who owes *you* an apology, Janet."

"I-I thought you were a thief." She pressed her hands to her blushing cheeks.

Wills crossed his arms. "No, you thought I was the thief."

"Well, yes." She couldn't look at him.

"Mike, I'm trying to explain here," the minister spoke up.

"Sorry."

"Janet, your father's buried money wasn't a secret. Everyone in town knew about it. He didn't steal it from his bank, like some have done in these hard times. He sold your mother's jewelry. The money was hidden for you. To care for you as you, ah, grew older as a single woman."

Janet's blush deepened. "He thought . . . The whole town thought I would never marry."

"He wasn't very smart, was he," Wills said.

"Pardon me?" Janet's temper rose.

The minister held up both hands to stop the anger. "Let me finish, please. As I said, the town knew about the money. The rumor got to the hobo camp. That was why I asked Mike to keep an eye on you."

"You sent him?" Janet looked from the pastor to Mike.

Reed nodded, but groaned. He pressed the towel to his head. "He wasn't starting his job until the first of the month. He had the time, and you had the need."

"I needed a gardener," she whispered.

"No, you needed a guard," Wills corrected her.

She glared at him. "You mean my money needed a guard." She turned her anger on the pastor. "How did you know where it was? Why were you digging it up?"

"Your father told me about it. He asked me to watch out for you. The money put you at risk, Janet. Mike is going to keep it in his safe."

"His safe? Where would that be?"

"At the jail, of course. He's our new town sheriff."

Now Janet was really mad. Both of the men had taken it upon themselves to control her life. They hadn't even talked to her. They just acted. She was insulted.

She glared at Wills. "You said you were a farmer," she snapped.

"I farmed with my dad. After a few years of college, I became a lawman." He shrugged those broad shoulders. His arms dropped to his sides. His face softened as his eyes searched her face. "And I like gardening."

Janet's heartbeat sped up. She swallowed then took a deep breath. "You said you were hungry when you came to my door."

THE GARDNER

Holding her gaze with his own, Mike lifted her hand. "I was. Your dad was right about one thing and wrong about another. Your cooking *is* county fair good. Maybe . . . well, maybe by fall we could enter both your cooking and my garden harvest in the county fair."

Janet shivered as his thumb circled the palm of the hand he held. "I guess we can talk about it. What, ah, was my father wrong about?"

That wonderful smile lit up his face. "He shouldn't have worried about someone wanting to marry you."

--The End—

THE GARDENER
GLOSSARY

ache – throbbing pain.

blink – to close and open the eyes.

blush – face turning red due to uneasy feeling.

bother – to cause trouble or upset.

bragging – trying to impress others about skill, knowledge, or status

breeze – a light wind.

canned – putting cooked food in jars to make it last a long time.

college – school of higher learning beyond high school.

curtain – cloth that hangs down to cover a doorway or window.

forehead -- the top part of a person's face between the hair line and the eyes.

gardener – a person who plants and works on a garden

glare – a harsh stare when someone is angry or doesn't like something.

grab – to take a hold by force.

THE GARDNER

hobo – homeless, out-of-work people camping out and begging

insult – to say bad things about someone.

interrupt – to jump in and stop talk or action.

jewelry – rings, earrings, necklaces, bracelets word as decoration, sometimes made of gems and gold or silver.

manly – looking or acting like a strong man.

murmur – to speak softly.

nibble – to eat in very small bites.

pastor – a minister of a church.

polite – using good manners that show respect for others.

potato or potatoes – a root vegetable.

pry – to ask about someone else's business.

relief – happiness that something bad is over.

risk – possible injury from danger.

ruffles – a narrow line of gathered cloth used a decoration.

shovel – a tool with a long handle and a metal scoop used for digging.

shrug -- raise or lift the shoulders, meaning "I don't care."

taxes – money demanded by city, state, country to pay for services.

twinkle – sparkle or glitter like blinking lights.

ugly – not pretty.

THE GARDENER
MENTOR QUESTIONS

Q1. What had Janet's father told her about bums? How does this make her treat her visitors?

Q2. What kind of work did Mike offer to do? What does he expect as payment?

Q3. What kinds of things can Janet cook? What other kinds of work do you think she can do?

Q4. Mike asked questions about Janet's house and her money. Why did that worry her?

Q5. Who came to Janet's door when Mike wasn't there? What did they want? Why did they go away?

Q6. What did Janet do about the noise that awakened her? Who did she think it was?

Q7. How did everyone know about Janet's buried money? Was that a good or bad thing?

Q8. Janet said she needed a gardener, but Mike said she needed something else. What was that?

Q9. What was Mike's real job? What was he doing in the meantime?

Q10. Mike thought Janet's father had been right about one thing and wrong about another. What were those things? What do you think happened after the story?

THE GARDENER
POSSIBLE ANSWERS

A1. Before her father died he had warned her "Never talk to a bum. And don't feed one. That's like feeding a stray dog. He will keep coming back. You never know if he might hurt you or steal from you." This made Janet afraid and distrustful of strangers because she always expected the worst from them.

A2. He said he could do gardening and yard work because he had been a farmer. When she says she has no money to pay him he says a plate of food is good enough.

A3. The townspeople think her cooking is "country fair" good. Her ham and beans is considered her best dish. Mike is pleased with her fried potatoes and onion and her pancakes. She takes care of the house and canning of the garden stuff. She only knew how to plant potatoes until Mike showed her.

A4. Because of her father's warnings, Janet worried that Mike was asking questions about her business matters and the house to plan on stealing her money.

A5. Two rude men come to the back door. Their lack of good manners and demands for food make her nervous. They were a contrast to Mike's good manners and willingness to work for food. She doesn't want to tell them she is alone and is relieved when Mike shows up. His protectiveness hurries them on their way.

A6. She ran outside to stop the thief, thinking that it's Mike. She grabbed the shovel as a weapon and knocked Pastor Reed into the hole he was digging. Mike is upset she thought it was him and she's upset that they were making decisions about her money without talking to her first.

A7. Her father was well-liked in the town. He was seen as a good and honest banker. When everyone was losing money and he had to close the bank, he sold his wife's jewelry and buried it beside the cellar door, telling Pastor Reed about it so he could see that she was taken care of even as she became an aging Old Maid. The good thing was the entire town was really looking out for her, but the bad part was someone eventually shared the gossip with the homeless hobo camp putting her at risk of an attack by people who didn't care about her.

A8. When she said she needed a gardener, Mike said she needed a guard. She thinks he means a guard over her money, but he is more concerned for her safety.

A9. Pastor Reed tells her that Mie will put her money in "his safe." Thinking Mike is just a hobo, she demands to know what that means. The minister tells her Mike is their new town sheriff but won't start until the first of the month. He had asked Mike to offer to work for Janet to keep an eye on her until he took over his new job and could officially keep her money safe.

A10. Mikes says her father (and the town) was right that her cooking is county fair good. He wants to prove it to her by entering her cooking at the fall county fair along with the garden stuff he plans to grow. He goes on to tell her the man was wrong that no one would ever want to marry her. By how he protects her, looks at her, and touches her, Mike wants to marry her.

ROSES FOR ANNIE

A ROMANCE

"Do you have one dollar?" Paul asked.

Luke frowned. His twin brother had never asked for money. Paul didn't even know much about money. He had no need for it in the special home where he lived. Luke visited him three times a week. On Sundays he ate dinner with Paul. It was Sunday.

His brother had lived in the home for a long time. Their mother had cared for slow Paul until she died. It had been hard for Luke to pay other people to care for his brother. Paul had special needs. Those needs cost money.

Luke chose to make money for Paul. He left college to build houses. Half his pay went toward Paul's care. That didn't bother Luke. He had always loved his brother. And he had always felt a little guilty. He was normal and Paul wasn't.

"What do you need a dollar for?"

Paul leaned over his plate of food on the table. He bent his head. Thick brown hair fell across his brow.

His dark brown eyes looked from side to side. No one was near them in the dining room.

"It's a secret."

"Brothers tell each other secrets."

Paul chewed his lower lip. "I never had a secret to tell. Do you have one?"

Luke sighed. Yes, he did, but Paul wouldn't understand. "Dreams are like secrets, because you can only see your own. You see them when you are asleep or when you are thinking about them. Understand?"

Paul nodded. Luke didn't continue. Paul beat on his plate with his fork. He chanted, "Tell me . . . Tell me . . . Tell me."

Luke covered his brother's hand to stop the noise. "You first."

Paul took a deep breath. His eyes sparkled. His smile showed his excitement and happiness. "I have a new friend."

"Really?" Luke looked around the dining room. He saw the two old women in wheelchairs. They had lived in the home a long time before Paul came. Colorful new blankets covered their laps. One of the nurses sat between them. She gave each a bite of food. Another nurse held a napkin to a skinny man's chin. Coffee spilled from the cup in his hand. The hand shook too much. A girl at the next table laughed at the spill. The nurse said something to her.

"Is that girl with the round face your new friend?" Luke asked. "I don't know her."

"No. That's Karen," Paul said. "She doesn't stay at night. They take her home. But not tonight. She has to sleep here tonight."

"They?"

"Her family."

Luke's heart hurt. That was his dream. He wanted his brother to have a normal life. He wanted Paul to live with him again. It had been so long since they had been a family. "So, who is your new friend?"

"Annie. She comes every day. I think it's every day. Not at the same time, but every day. Yes, I think it's every day," Paul repeated.

Luke saw the confused look in Paul's eyes. Again he covered his hand. "Every day? She must be very nice."

"She is. That's why I need a dollar. A dollar for flowers. Annie likes flowers. She said so."

Luke frowned harder. His brother had never noticed girls before. He had the mind of an eight-year-old boy. Little boys didn't like little girls.

Twenty-four-year-old Luke had lots of girlfriends. The girls he dated were pretty. Looks were one thing. Kindness was another. Not one of Luke's girlfriends was kind enough to visit his brother. Normal girls like Luke's friends would not understand Paul.

Now Paul had a girlfriend? Why was she visiting him? Why was she telling him she liked flowers? Had she asked him to buy flowers for her? Luke knew he had to meet this Annie. She might hurt Paul. She might say unkind things that would hurt him. If she stopped coming, that would make Paul feel worse, but he didn't want him hurt.

He decided to talk to the man who ran the home. He should know about people who came here every day. He should be able to tell Luke about his brother's new friend.

Luke sat at the café counter. His coffee cup was empty. He didn't let the red-haired waitress fill it again. He hadn't ordered any food either. He waited.

The clock on the wall showed 4:25. Annie started work at 4:30. She was a waitress at the Garden Café. Mr. Kelly at the home didn't know anything else about her. He said she brought gifts and made people smile. She had started coming a month ago. She visited every day before going to work. Luke came to the café to find out why she did that.

He looked at the pictures of flowers on the walls. She worked around those pictures. Maybe that was why she had asked Paul to buy her real flowers. She shouldn't have asked though. That wasn't right. Smart people could get gifts or money from slow people like Paul. Then those smart people got busy with their own lives or moved on. They didn't really care.

Luke let the anger grow inside. Paul had to be protected from unkind people. Luke was not going to let this Annie hurt his brother.

A door opened. A short young woman came from the kitchen. Curly blonde hair fell around her face. Her green eyes sparkled. She was more than pretty. She was beautiful. Her name tag told him she was Annie.

Annie tied her apron in place. She laughed at the cook's joke as she pushed the door open with one hip. Her gaze fell on the man sitting at the counter. She stopped to look around. She didn't see any of the nurses from the home. She hurried forward.

"Paul! What are you doing here by yourself? How did you get here?"

The man didn't smile. He glared. "I'm not Paul. I'm his brother Luke."

"Oh! He didn't tell me . . . No one told me Paul had a twin brother."

"Does it make a difference?"

"What?"

"Does it make a difference that Paul has someone to protect him?"

"Protect him? Protect him from what?"

"Girls like you."

"Like me?" she asked. A blush spread up her neck and into her cheeks. "You think I'm a bad person?"

"I don't know. What I do know is that you asked Paul to spend money on you."

"I did not! Who told you that?"

"Paul did."

She closed her eyes. After a deep breath, she opened her eyes again. No, this man did not look like Paul. Paul's eyes were a warm chocolate brown. Luke's eyes were as hard as frozen mud.

Paul was happy. He enjoyed every simple thing. The silky fur of a tiny kitten. Laughter. The smell of new-cut grass. The changing shapes of fluffy clouds.

MEETING PEOPLE

Luke looked too unhappy to understand those simple things.

"I never asked Paul for anything money could buy," she said. "I don't care if you believe me. I feel sorry for you. You will never understand your brother. Now, I have work to do. Were you going to order?"

Luke pushed his coffee cup aside. "No. I came to see what you were like. What do you want from my brother?"

"Nothing, except to enjoy being with him. What is your point with that question?"

Luke shook his head. He didn't believe her. "Paul thinks like an eight-year-old boy. What could a beautiful woman want with him? Do you pity him? Do you come back here and tell stories about him? Do you make fun of him?"

"I've heard enough. Please leave."

Luke slid off the stool and stood up. He had to be over six feet tall to tower over her. He pointed a finger. The finger almost poked her in the breast. She stepped back. Her heartbeat sped up.

"Stay away from Paul," he ordered in a low voice. Then he turned toward the door.

"You can't boss me around!" she yelled.

The door slammed shut behind him. Luke left the café but not Annie's thoughts. *Had he called her beautiful?*

Paul stopped talking about Annie. Luke thought she had listened to his order not to visit the home.

It rained hard one day. Luke couldn't build houses in the rain. He went to visit Paul. That was the day he found out Annie hadn't listened to him.

Luke walked down the hallway to his brother's room. His brother was not there. The TV was off. His bed was neatly made. A kitten lay curled in a ball in the middle of the bed. It was asleep. Luke couldn't remember animals in the home. He hoped Paul wasn't breaking any rules and hiding it. He didn't want his brother kicked out. He would have to talk to him. First he had to find him.

Luke stood in the hallway. He frowned. He couldn't hear anyone or any TV in the other rooms. He walked to the nurse's desk. No one was there either. He heard laughter and clapping hands. The sounds came from the dining room.

"Paul! Paul! Paul!" voices chanted.

Luke peaked around the doorway. He blinked. The tables had been pushed back. The home was having a party.

Paul stood in the middle of the circle of chairs and wheelchairs. Luke counted. He had never seen all eleven people in the dining room at the same time. Some always wanted to stay in their rooms at meal time. The nurses had told him they didn't like company. They didn't like to talk to anyone except their families.

But that day they had all come together to play. Paul had a colorful beach ball. They called for him to throw it. They laughed. They clapped.

The nurses stood back watching. Someone ran around behind the eleven patients. Paul turned. Then Luke saw who wanted him to throw the ball.

MEETING PEOPLE

Annie. Annie with the curly hair and green eyes. Annie who had all the people in the home laughing. She stopped behind one of the old ladies in a wheelchair. She waved her hands.

Paul threw the ball to the old lady.

"I caught it!" the old woman shouted then giggled like a girl.

"Emma caught it!"

"You are good, Emma!"

"Throw it high for me," Paul shouted.

She did.

"Paul! Paul! Paul!" the voices chanted again.

"One more, then it's time for the two cakes that I brought," Annie called out. She skipped to a place behind the shaky old man.

Luke had never seen the old man smile. Now a broad grin made wrinkles in his face. The old man caught the ball. His shaky hands pushed it up to Annie. She kissed one of the hands. The old man patted her cheek.

Luke backed away from the doorway. He walked slowly to Paul's room. He sat on the bed for a long time. Shame washed over him. He had thought Annie was after something. She came just to give joy. She gave time. She gave herself to the people living in the home. She made Paul laugh.

On Monday Annie hurried from the café kitchen to the counter, then from the kitchen to the tables. She carried many plates of food. She smiled and thanked the people who ate at the café. She was too busy to see the two men come in the door.

The talking and eating stopped. Annie looked around. Paul and Luke stood side by side. They smiled the same smile. The brown eyes in the two handsome faces were the color of warm chocolate. Annie's heart beat hard and fast.

"Here." Paul held out a dozen pink roses. The blooms were so big and beautiful.

"Paul said pink was your favorite color," Luke said.

She took a breath. It was hard to do. Her throat felt tight. Tears filled her eyes.

"Thank you. Both of you," she whispered.

Luke stepped forward. "No. I'm the one thanking *you*. You made my brother happy. You just wanted to be nice, to be kind. I never knew a girl who would do that."

"Are you going to kiss her, young man?" someone asked.

Annie blushed. Paul poked his brother's arm.

"No." Luke looked around at all the people smiling at them. He shrugged. "At least not yet."

--The End—

MEETING PEOPLE

ROSES FOR ANNIE
GLOSSARY

beautiful – very nice to look at, more than pretty.

believe – to know something is true.

blink – to close and open eyes.

blonde – pale yellow to gold colored hair or someone having that color hair.

blush – face turning red due to uneasy feeling.

bother – to cause trouble or upset.

caught – to catch something.

chocolate – a sweet brown treat or candy.

college – school of higher learning beyond high school.

counter – top of a table or cabinet, long surface in a café where people can sit.

difference – being unlike something else or changing.

excitement -- showing great happiness or interest.

glare – a harsh stare when someone is angry or doesn't like something.

guilty – feeling badly for something.

handsome – good looking or pleasing to look at.

kindness – saying something or doing something just to make others feel good.

pity – feeling sorry for someone.

protect – guard or save.

short – below how tall others are or not long enough.

silky – feeling smooth to the touch, like silk cloth.

shrug – lifting of the shoulders to show something doesn't matter.

sparkle – shiny, catching light.

waitress – a woman who works in a restaurant taking orders and bringing food to people.

MEETING PEOPLE

ROSES FOR ANNIE
MENTOR QUESTIONS

Q1. Paul asked his brother for what? Why?

Q2. What kind of secrets did each of the brothers have?

Q3. Why was Luke angry with Annie? Do you think he was right? Why or Why not?

Q4. Where did Luke go to talk to Annie? Why did he want to meet her?

Q5. What did Annie think when she saw Luke? Why? How did Luke make her feel?

Q6. What were the people doing at the home when Luke visited on the rainy day? What was Paul doing? How did that make Luke feel?

Q7. Why do you think Annie was visiting the home? Why did she ignore Luke's orders?

Q8. How was Annie different from the other normal girls Luke knew?

Q9. What did Luke do with Paul after the party? How did he change?

Q10. What do you think happens to Luke, Paul, and Annie after the story?

ROSES FOR ANNIE
POSSIBLE ANSWERS

A1. Paul wanted Luke to give him a dollar to buy flowers for his new friend Annie.

A2. Paul has been at the special care home for a long time so he is happy to have a new friend. Luke feels guilty that he is normal and his twin is slow needing special care. His secret dream is to have his brother living with him again as a family.

A3. Luke thought Annie was taking advantage of Paul being slow and asking him to buy her flowers. Special needs people are easily manipulated and easily believe what they are told. It is important for relatives and care givers to pay attention to special needs visitors to protect the slow people.

A4. Luke went to the café where he was told Annie worked. He wanted to find out what kind of girl she was to be visiting a special needs home. He wanted to tell her to stay away from his brother.

A5. Annie at first thought Luke was Paul because they were twins who looked so much alike. She thought Paul had left the care of the special needs home to visit her and that worried her. She was insulted when Luke accused her of taking advantage of Paul. She doesn't try to explain anything because he is so angry.

A6. The staff had all of the smiling residents in a circle with Paul in the middle and Annie running around the outside of the circle. Paul was laughing, playing the game of tossing the ball to whoever Annie stood behind. Annie tells them she brought two cakes for them to share. Luke is surprised at everyone's laughing participation and Annie's determination to make them happy. He returns to Paul's room to rethink his opinion of her.

MEETING PEOPLE

A7. Annie didn't have a lot of money because she worked as a waitress. She was new to the town. Something in her past made her want to spend time and effort at the special needs home to simply spread joy, fun, and smiles. She has a basically generous spirit who cares for the less fortunate and elderly. She saw Luke as being over-bearing and not understanding all the blessing Paul can experience. She understands Paul so she chooses to ignore Luke's orders.

A8. Luke's normal girlfriends seem to be selfish and shallow only caring about themselves and feeling uncomfortable around people who aren't normal. Annie is the exact opposite. She is surprised Luke calls her beautiful and the happiness of others makes her happy. She willingly spends her time and money on a regular basis at the special needs home getting to know the people as unique individuals living their lives, not as people who need to be set aside and forgotten.

A9. Luke takes Paul with him to deliver the pink roses he bought for Annie. His heart is more open and he is more aware of how to make Paul happy.

A10. Since Luke thinks Annie is beautiful and admires her generosity and Annie thinks he is handsome and loves his twin so much, it is very possible that they will eventually share that kiss and maybe create a home Paul can live in with the two of them taking care of him.

SANTA'S HELPER, OR NOT

A ROMANCE

Mary Michelle Crump closed her eyes. She didn't want to look at the clock on the wall across from her counter. The past month had made her hate clocks.

"You will not move," she ordered the minute hand. Her unhappy wish did not stop the timed lock on the mall doors. She opened her eyes on the clock. It was 8:00 a.m.

The Trevor doors slid open. The mall was open. A mob of people entered. Most of them were women with their winter coats open. They had red-faces from the winter wind outside the mall. They looked like runners in a race.

The Christmas shoppers burst through the store's open doors. The loud speakers in the mall played a noisy holiday song. It was not "We Wish You a Merry Christmas."

Mary sighed. She dropped her lipstick into her open purse. It sat in the bottom drawer below her cash register. She kicked the drawer closed.

Twice she tried to smile. Finally it froze in place. Five women moved toward her lingerie displays. Two of the women looked at lists. Two others stopped at the nighty display. Mary heard them giggle. The last one frowned at the bra-and-panty sets on the sale table. Mary decided to greet her first. Maybe she could get her to smile. Maybe she couldn't. She headed to the sale table.

Two hours later Mary wanted to scream. She glanced up. Nine impatient customers waited for her. They held items they wanted to buy.

Mary was the only clerk in sight. Mona-the-college-girl was in the dressing rooms. Mary hoped she was really helping the upset woman she sent to her. The only other clerk was on break. *Who knows when that one will be seen again.* She sighed.

A crash sounded followed by screams. Beyond the sale table and racks of nightgowns, the wall display fell. Mary slammed the cash drawer shut. She joined the crowd rushing to the disaster.

Three teenage girls climbed out of the mess. They pushed aside red and green satin and lace that had been on the wall. Mary shoved to the front of the curious crowd. She scanned the girls' faces, arms, and legs. The teens looked angry. All body parts seemed in working order with no blood showing. All three girls glared at their watchers.

"Sharon did it!"

"I did not. That stupid chair tipped over. I grabbed the panties off the hook."

"You should have left them alone. You are the stupid one!"

"They match my dress!"

"You mean your red face, don't you?"

"Girls!" Mary shouted over them. "Be quiet! Are any of you hurt?"

"No."

"My elbow hurts."

"My hair caught on something."

Mary looked at the mess. She put her hands on her hips. She wanted to grab and shake the girls, one by one. "Isn't that just awful," she snapped. "That's what you get for skipping school."

The guilty girls blinked at her. She heard people talking behind her. Somebody said she was being rude to her customers. Another person called her mean. Several said they were taking their money someplace else.

The head clerk stepped to her side. "What on earth is going on? Miss Crump, help those girls."

"Help them do what, Miss Angelus? Tear down another display or out the door?"

"Well, I never . . . ." the aging woman's mouth dropped open. Under her sad, blonde wig, her fat face reddened. She always wore too much eye shadow. Those eyes glared at Mary. "See that the college girl rebuilds this display. She's more artistic than you. Go back to your counter and your customers. I will help these poor girls and talk to you later."

"I'm sure you will," Mary muttered. Miss Angelus looked even madder.

As she walked, Mary worked on her dignity. *Why can't you keep your mouth shut? You need this second job. Your car is dead and the rent's due. You have one cheap present bought for Chrissy. That's probably more than her mother has done. Forget her father-the-jerk.*

"Miss, I really would like to pay for this . . . if you are still working here," someone said.

"I'm sorry, ma'am, I--" She hit her leg on the open drawer under her register. Mary bent down to rub her leg. She stared into the very empty drawer.

"No, no!" she moaned. "It's gone."

"What's gone?" Miss Angelus asked. "Stand up. You have customers."

Mary's leg hurt as she came to her feet. "My purse. It was in the drawer."

"Which is against the rules. We have lockers."

"For a five dollar deposit I couldn't pay."

A customer spoke up. "These high prices at Trevor's and you can't pay fair wages? I'm going somewhere else."

Miss Angelus gritted her teeth. "Now see what you've done!"

"You asked what happened!"

A male voice asked, "I don't think the initials M.C. stand for Merry Christmas. Ho-ho-ho."

Mary turned to look into a pair of bright blue eyes above a wide smile. A handsome man stood on the other side of her counter. He was too tall to be Saint Nick. His hair and close beard were dark red instead of white. A thrill shot from Mary's chest into her stomach. She wet her lips and clenched her hands.

He winked at her. "I think they stand for Mary Crump, don't they?"

A roar filled her ears. Miss Angelus and the store faded away as she looked into those eyes. The world returned when Miss Angelus poked her in the back. She blinked. The man wore a uniform. He was a mall cop. And he held her missing purse in one hand and a crying teen girl in the other.

Mary stared at the purse. The buckle had been ripped away but her initials had been stamped on the flap.

"You billfold's inside. I grabbed her in the doorway. She stopped to get to your money."

"What little there is," Mary whispered.

She reached for the purse. Their fingers touched. Their eyes met again. His smile turned smug. Did he know how she felt? She grabbed the purse. He cleared his throat and looked at her boss.

"Miss Angelus, this girl is one of a gang. They played the same game at Beren's but got into a cash drawer left open. Miss Crump didn't let that happen here. The girl stole her purse instead."

"And you returned it to her." The wig bobbed as Miss Angelus nodded. "You are a very good mall guard. I will tell your brother, Mr. Crosby."

He waved his one free hand. "Not needed. But you might do me a favor. Miss Crump looks like she could use a break. Since the police are on their way, I would like to take Miss Crump for a hot chocolate."

Miss Angelus glanced at the customers watching and listening. "How nice. If she is willing and . . . has the time." Her tone sounded like Mary should stay here.

"So are you?" The blue-eyed guard looked Mary.

"What?"

"Willing and have the time?"

Mary needed to sit down. She glanced at Miss Angelus. "I-I have work to do, people waiting. Busy season, you know."

The guard smiled sadly, nodded, and left with the teen firmly in hand.

Fifteen minutes later, Mary counted change for an old woman. Someone tugged on her skirt.

"Thank you," the old woman said. She stretched to look over the counter. "I think one of Santa's elves needs your help."

Mary looked down. Her five-year-old niece looked up at her. Black curls crowded from the hood of her too-small coat. Her big brown eyes had tears.

"Chrissy! You shouldn't be behind the counter. Where's your mother?"

A mitten held up a note. "Mama said I am to sit where you put me. And be quiet. I can whisper stories to Amy." She held a dirty rag doll under her other arm.

Mary groaned but took the note. It read "Job interview. S.C. Associates. Stock brokers. They are desperate and so am I. One hour. Sorry. Beth."

"Perfect. How can I look after a kid at work?"

"She didn't want me to go with her. Now you don't want me." Chrissy backed up. Tears slipped down her face. "I told her you wouldn't want me."

Mary went to her knees. Her thumb wiped at the tears. "Not true. It's just . . ." *How could she explain to a small child?*

SANTA'S HELPER, OR NOT

"Mama said she had to go. Because Daddy doesn't want us, either. Nobody wants me!" The little girl ran for the door to the mall.

"Miss, you sold me damaged goods. Is that why they were on the sale table?" Her first customer of the day was back.

"Mona!" The red-headed college clerk stepped to the counter. Mary gave the customer a smile, took the Trevor's sack from her, and handed it to Mona. "Make this woman happy. I'm going on break. I don't know for how long."

Mary ran out the door looking for Chrissy. She fought her panic. She let anger wash over her. She was angry at everything and everyone. Her soon to be ex-brother-in-law for leaving his family two weeks before Christmas. Her demanding sister. The nasty shoppers. And her crying niece who made her feel guilty. She was also mad at herself for acting like a crazy woman. She pushed people aside as she frantically searched for Chrissy.

Chrissy stood in front of the mall's Santa Workshop. "Thank goodness!" Mary gasped then stopped.

Mr. Crosby was on his knees in front of the little girl. He nodded and wiped a tear from her cheek. Chrissy's little arm went around his neck. They shared a quick hug. Mary blinked at the look of pure joy on Mr. Crosby's face.

A moment later he was back to being a mall guard. He glanced around. He saw Mary. His instant smile made her gasp. He turned Chrissy and pointed at her. The little girl shyly nodded then ducked behind him.

He stood, Chrissy's hand in his. Mary walked toward them. Her heart raced.

"First your purse and now your child. That's two times. What do they say? Third time's a charm?"

Mary cleared her dry throat. "Chrissy is my niece. My sister left her here to go to a job interview."

"Just dropped her off?" He sounded angry. "Does she do that often? This is a child, not a puppy."

Mary glared at him. "Her husband walked out two weeks ago. My sister jumps at any job she can."

One broad palm came up to stop her angry words. "Sounds reasonable. Do you think she'll get the job?"

Mary frowned at him. She saw Chrissy lean against his leg and stare up at him like he was Santa. "How hard can it be to answer phones? Especially for a stock broker? One desperate for help at this time of year? She's pretty and smart. Why shouldn't she get it?"

"Runs in the family does it?" His eyes twinkled. He raised one eyebrow as he looked into Mary's eyes.

A blush crawled up her neck. She felt embarrassed. That made her angry again. "And what business is it of yours?"

The broad shoulders shrugged. "I guess none, if you don't want it to be." He looked at the very expensive watch on his wrist. "I'm passing time, waiting for Santa." He looked over her head. "And here he comes. Chrissy, you are first up. Then your Aunt Mary can sit on his lap."

"No-no-no!" Mary held up both hands.

Chrissy peeked around the blue uniformed leg. "Oh, please, Aunt Mary. I haven't talked to him yet.

SANTA'S HELPER, OR NOT

It's only . . ." Those big brown eyes looked up at her new hero. "How long did you say?"

"Two days," Crosby whispered.

"Two days," Chrissy whispered, too. "Please?"

"Of course you can sit on Santa's lap. I meant I wasn't going to do it."

"Why not? You are poorer than Mama and me. You must have a list this long." Chrissy held her arms wide. She almost dropped the Amy doll. Crosby caught it.

Mary's blush heated her face. She glanced round. She would not look at Crosby. "Chrissy, Santa fills children's needs. Grownups take care of their own."

"Ho-ho-ho!" boomed the Santa voice. "Is that my first visitor, Samson?"

"Yes, sir. Fate made Chrissy and her aunt come to this spot just in time," Crosby said.

Chrissy tugged on the dark blue pant leg. Crosby looked down. "What's fate? Is your name Samson? That's Aunt Mary's favorite Bible person. She says he was big and strong and handsome."

"Chrissy!" Mary turned the little girl to face Santa's chair. The man in the red suit waved. "Go talk to Santa."

"No."

"What's wrong now?"

Chrissy leaned closed to her aunt. "I'm not supposed to talk to strangers."

Mary frowned. "You sat on his knee last year."

"I sat on one knee and Mama sat on his other."

Crosby bent down. "There's a line now. Give in, Aunt Mary."

MEETING PEOPLE

A shiver shot down Mary's back. She jumped up, bumping him. When she gasped she smelled his aftershave. His hand pressed on her back. He pushed her to follow Chrissy. The little girl crawled onto a waiting knee. She looked back at Mary and pointed to Santa's other knee. With Crosby right behind her, she had no choice. She slowly sat, her eyes on the chattering Chrissy.

This is crazy! How dare the man! Chrissy is a little user. Well, I can play the game, too.

"Just three things, Chrissy?" Santa asked.

The little girl shrugged. "Mama said so. Now, it's Aunt Mary's turn. She needs a lot because she's alone. Christmas makes her grouchy."

Mary groaned. "No, it makes me tired. Working two jobs at Christmas makes me tired, Santa."

"And grouchy," Chrissy repeated.

Santa laughed. Crosby coughed.

Santa looked her in the eye. "So what can I bring you? What does a hard working and pretty young woman want?"

Mary frowned. Behind the glasses, Santa's eyes twinkled. "I think this mall has more than one nice man, Santa. I wonder if you are a miracle worker, too?" She leaned closer to whisper, "I work until close on Christmas Eve. My car died. I want a car to take me from work to church."

It was Santa's turn to frown. "Is that all?"

"Oh, I could ask for a gift for each of the twelve days of Christmas. No, all I really want is that ride."

Santa glanced at Chrissy then Crosby. He cleared his throat. "We'll have to see what can be done."

"We?" Chrissy asked, her eyes big. "You mean your elves, too?"

"Santa has lots of helpers, Chrissy," Crosby said for him. He lifted the little girl from Santa's knee. "And waiting customers."

Mary stood as he reached for her. She didn't want to risk his touch but forgot her hurt leg. It bent. Crosby's hands came to her waist to steady her. When he didn't let go right away, Mary looked into his blue eyes. Her breath caught. She pulled away to take Chrissy's hand.

"Santa's not the only one with waiting customers. I have to get back to work. Come on, Chrissy."

"Let her stay at the Lost and Found desk with me," Crosby quickly offered.

Chrissy jumped up and down. "I'll be good, Aunt Mary. And Amy will be quiet. Please?"

Later, a happy Beth pounded on her sister's counter. She had gotten the job at S. C. Associates. She would be answering phones and opening the mail. The company had a day care, too. It would be the perfect place to work. She headed to the Lost and Found to get Chrissy and share her good news.

Mary ate lunch at a hot dog stand. She didn't see Crosby's red hair and blue uniform among the shoppers. She told herself she wasn't looking for him.

When she walked into the mall the next day, Mary saw a flash of blue. She almost waved. The short, bald man was not Crosby. She had no time to keep looking. The Christmas Eve last minute shoppers kept her too busy.

At 9:15 p.m. a voice over the loud speakers said Trevor's would be closing in fifteen minutes. Mary cleaned her area. At 9:30 p.m. she tried not to cry as she went through her closing check list.

Her back ached, as well as the leg she had hurt the day before. Her last customer had happily told her a heavy snow fell outside. The city would have a beautiful white Christmas. Mary planned to walk the many blocks to her church. Now she had heavy snow to make that trip hard. She so needed the church service of candles, music, and hope.

"Hope?" she muttered as she closed her cash drawer. She sealed the money envelope, signed it, and handed it to the waiting Miss Angelus. They did not exchange a "Merry Christmas" like the co-workers around them. Mary Michelle Crump was too tired and grouchy.

"Miss Crump?" a voice said behind her.

Mary sighed before turning. A man in a dark suit with a cap on his head smiled at her. She looked past him to Trevor's closed doors.

"I'm sorry, sir. The mall and this store are closed."

"I'm not here to buy anything. I'm here to take you to church."

"What?"

Miss Angelus put her coat on her shoulders, handed over her torn purse, and waved her toward the man. He swept his hand toward the employee door. Mary frowned at him then at the also smiling Miss Angelus.

"Mary, you may find M.C. stands for Merry Christmas after all. Don't ask questions. Just enjoy."

Mary's frown stayed on her face. She held the man's arm as they went out the mall doors. Big snowflakes fell from low clouds. The man carefully walked her through the white stuff. He stopped at a very long, cream-colored car parked at the curb. The man opened the car door for her.

Mary bent to look into the dim light inside the big car. Dark red hair moved under the light. A man's gloved hand reached toward her.

"Third time to the rescue," a deep voice said. "That means this third time is charmed."

"Mr. Crosby? What is all this?"

"Get in. It's warmer in here and dry. A church service awaits."

Mary looked at the suited man still holding the car door then frowned at the handsome and bearded face looking at her from the car. "Did you hear me with Santa? And how can a mall guard rent a big car like this?"

The suited man coughed then took her elbow to move her forward into the car. The door closed. Crosby pulled off one glove to brush the snow from her hair.

Mary jerked her head away. "Stop that. You should not have done this. It costs way too much."

Crosby settled back in his seat to look her over. In the dim light of the big car, Mary saw he now wore a very nice coat, open over a fine suit. A silly reindeer smiled at her from his very red tie. The man's smile turned into a grin as the car stated to move. Mary glanced into the mirror. The man in the small cap winked back at her.

MEETING PEOPLE

"I have the address, Miss Crump," the driver said.

Mary looked back at Crosby. She shook her head. "What address?"

"You asked Santa for a ride to your church. Here we are. But, that wish is low on the miracle scale." Crosby took off his other glove. Then he lifted a large ribbon-tied box from the seat running up the side of the long car. He set the box in her lap. "This might be better."

Mary ran her fingertip over the shiny paper on the box. "You are not a mall guard."

"My brother owns the company. He was a man short. I owed him a favor. He made me work it off. He thinks we're even, but . . . ." Crosby sighed and stared into her eyes. "I think I owe him a lot more now. Open your Christmas present, Mary Crump."

Heart pounding, Mary untied the ribbon. She parted the paper and lifted the box lid. Tissue paper surrounded a beautiful egg. The car's dim light shone off its shell of purple, gold, and colored jewels. A tiny door lay open. Inside the egg was a tiny gold wire tree with little green jewels. In the tree sat a tiny bird made out of glittering white jewels.

"Oh, my!" Mary breathed. "This can't be for me. Are those stones real?" She pointed at the bird and its tree.

"You mean the Partridge in the Pear Tree? It's made of diamonds. The tree is spun gold with little emeralds as pears."

Mary's eyes widened. She glanced at him then back at the egg. "Who made . . . Where did you . . . Why?" she finally demanded.

He looked at the very expensive watch she remembered. "It is a couple of hours before the First Day of Christmas, but old S.C. just couldn't wait to give it to you."

"S.C. as in Santa Claus?"

"No, as in me, Samson Crosby, owner of S.C. Associates. Yes, where your sister Beth now works. I'm a broker, investor, partner in my brother's companies. I'm also a lonely single guy, but I think fate is going to take care of that. I hope so, anyway."

"Hope?"

He took Mary's hand in his. "Hope is what Christmas is all about, isn't it? You and I can talk about the hope that is 'Love at First Sight.' Hope that is a Partridge in a Pear Tree so you and I remember this Christmas night forever. We can move on to the rest of the Twelve Days of Christmas, turning hope into reality. Maybe Day Two turtle doves in the Cayman Islands then Paris for French hens, calling birds in the Alps—"

Mary leaned forward. Her fingers pressed against his lips to stop him. "Your hope is running way too fast. I can't keep up. This is all too much. You are a stranger. I don't know you."

He kissed her fingers and grinned at her shiver. "Exactly my point. We will need every minute of the next twelve days. Tonight we can start with church and that Partridge."

"Mr. Crosby—"

"Call me S.C. Mary Michelle Crump, I will give you twelve days of the most exciting, fun-filled, and carefree days of your life. Not once will you feel tired or grouchy. That was Chrissy's wish when she said I had to be Santa's helper to make you smile."

"Chrissy? That's not fair."

"Please. Give us a chance." He cupped her face. "Give me these days to talk, to share my hopes, listen to your hopes, to think about a future together. I know you are a good person. I want that goodness in my life. No, I need that goodness and everything else about you. I want to kiss and honor you. I want to give you the world so you will be willing and have time for me on that Twelfth Day."

"Time for you then? Where did you plan for us to be on that Twelfth Day?" she whispered. Her mind buzzed in awe of this sweet man working so hard to win her heart.

"First Methodist Church. Beth already has it booked." He looked like a hopeful little boy staring in the window of a toy store.

She could hardly breathe. "The first time you asked if I would be willing and have time for hot chocolate in the mall. Are you absolutely sure S.C. doesn't stand for Santa Claus?"

He took a quick, hopeful breath. "It could be if you let M.C. stand for—"

Mary smiled up at him. "Merry Christmas or Mary Crosby?"

Crosby pulled her into his arms for a wonderful kiss that could take them into twelve days and even a lifetime.

--The End--

SANTA'S HELPER, OR NOT
GLOSSARY

aftershave – good smelling stuff men put on their face after shaving.

Alps – mountains in Europe that run through several countries like France and Italy.

artistic – knowing how to make something look pleasing.

Associates – a group of business people working together.

awful – event or feeling that is bad.

billfold – a small folding case for carrying money, cards, and I.D.

blonde – yellow colored hair.

buckle – a metal circle a strap goes through to hold something in place.

cash register – the machine where people punch keys to enter sales and store money.

Cayman Islands – islands in the Atlantic Ocean with fancy hotels.

chatter – talking very fast.

check list – a person's list of work that has to be marked when done.

choice – when a person decides on an action or takes special items from many.

clench – tight hand hold.

college – harder school after high school.

curious – wanting to understand or know about something.

damaged – badly made or torn things

demanding – wanting things or actions right now.

deposit – a little money paid to hold or rent something.

desperate – wanting something very badly.

dignity – feeling proud of self around other people.

disaster – event that is very bad.

embarrassed – feeling badly that one did something.

emeralds – green jewels that cost a lot of money.

exciting – feeling stirred up wanting something to happen.

expensive – costing a lot of money.

Fate – thinking actions are made to happen for a reason.

frantic – moving quickly with bad feelings that something won't get done.

SANTA'S HELPER, OR NOT

glare – a mean look at something or someone.

grab -- to quickly take hold.

grit or gritted – clamping teeth together.

grouchy – feeling badly and talking in short, angry words to keep from being bothered.

guilty – feeling badly for an action done or not done.

handsome – looks that are pleasing or very nice.

impatient – feeling in a hurry.

initials – first letters of a person's name or a business instead of using complete names.

interview – talking to someone wants a job or to learn about a person.

jewels – clear real stones from the earth that cost a lot or fake colored glass to look like them.

lingerie – a woman's underwear, usually lacy and pretty.

miracle -- a happening that no one ever expected.

miracle worker – a person who makes miracles happen.

nasty – unhappy and rude actions or bad tasting.

niece – girl child of a person's sister or brother.

nighty – another word for night gown, usually short and lacy.

panic – feeling trapped and in fear of something bad happening.

Partridge (in a Pear Tree) – a fat little bird that doesn't fly very well.

reasonable – knowing something will work or sounds right.

reindeer – a short deer with horns who some think pulls Santa Claus's sleigh.

skipping – choosing to not go (as in skipping school) or uneven beat or step.

smug – looking too happy about being right or with someone's reaction.

stock broker – a trained person who invests money in businesses.

stranger – a person never met before and know nothing about.

stretch – reaching more than a person normally does.

uniform – special clothes worn for a job, such as a police uniform

SANTA'S HELPER, OR NOT
MENTOR QUESTIONS

Q1. How did Mary feel about Christmas shoppers? What did she do about the ones who were rude?

Q2. Why did Mary work? Did you ever find out what her second job was?

Q3. What did the teenage girls do in the store?

Q4. Why was Chrissy in the store? How did the little girl feel about being there?

Q5. Where did Chrissy go when she ran away and who was there? What was his name and what was he called?

Q6. What did Chrissy say to Santa about Mary? How did that make Mary feel? What did Mary ask for from Santa?

Q7. Why do you think Mary's boss, Miss Angelus, changed toward Mary?

Q8. What Christmas present(s) did Crosby give Mary? How could he afford all that? How did that relate to Christmas and what was happening between them?

Q9. How did Chrissy and her mother Beth help Crosby surprise Mary?

Q10. According to the story what are some of the things the letters S.C and M.C. stand for?

SANTA'S HELPER, OR NOT
POSSIBLE ANSWERS

A1. Mary felt frustrated, angry, overworked, impatient. She tried hard to put a smile on her face and treat everyone with good manners. She did get sarcastic with the teenage girls, though.

A2. She was poor and had to work two jobs. Her car had died, her rent was due, and she had not bought all her Christmas presents for her niece and her sister. We never heard about her first job, just that working the two jobs had exhausted her.

A3. They pulled a display from the wall, made a mess, screamed a lot, and attracted attention so the one girl could get to the cash register. Mary had locked the register before leaving her counter, so the only thing the girls could do was steal Mary's purse. We found out they had pulled the same stunt before. This time the mall guard had caught the thief and the police were on their way.

A4. Mary's sister Beth dropped off Chrissy at the door with a note to Mary that she had to go on a job interview and couldn't take Chrissy with her. Chrissy felt like nobody wanted her. Her father had left the family two weeks before, her mother leaves her with her aunt, and the aunt doesn't want her at the store.

A5. Chrissy ran from her aunt's store and out into the mall. She ran to Santa's Workshop where Samson Crosby, the handsome mall guard, stops and talks to her. Mary arrives then Santa. When Santa calls the guard Samson, Chrissy points out that's her aunt's favorite Bible character. Embarrassed, Mary only refers to him as Mr. Crosby. It's not until his surprise that he tells her who he really is as the owner of the stock brokerage, S.C. Associations and most people call him S.C.

MEETING PEOPLE

A6. With Crosby eavesdropping, Chrissy tells Santa that Mary is poor and works two jobs. She says she is always tired and grouchy. When asked what she wants for Christmas, Mary says she could ask for something for each of the Twelve Days of Christmas, but all she really wants is a ride to Christmas Eve church services.

A7. Miss Angelus knows Crosby is working for his brother. When he asked her to let Mary go on break with him, she hints to Mary that she had customers and shouldn't go. However, when the driver shows up to give Mary a ride to church, Miss Angelus goes to the employee locker room and brings back Mary's coat and purse. She tells Mary not to ask questions and just enjoy a "Merry Christmas." Crosby could have told her how rich and influential he really was and that makes Miss Angelus treat Mary nicer.

A8. As owner of the stock brokerage and other companies, Crosby provided the limo to drive Mary to church as she asked Santa, but since he has money and is "suffering" from Love-at-first-sight, he also has plans to fulfill her hinted wish for gifts on each of the Twelve Days of Christmas. He starts with the gold and gem decorated egg with a Partridge in a Pear Tree. Then he tells her he wants to take her to fancy places like the Cayman Islands, Paris, and the Alps. He wants to end up on the Twelfth Day at her church that her sister has already booked for their wedding. At first stunned and skeptical, Mary gradually comes around and accepts his proposal.

A9. Crosby had obviously questioned the five year old Chrissy about her aunt. He then recruited her sister as his new employee to make all the arrangements for him.

A10. S.C. are the initials for Santa Claus, for Crosby's company S.C. Associates, and for the man himself, Samson Crosby. M.C. are Mary Crumps' initials but also stand for Merry Christmas and she tells Crosby they could also stand for Mary Crosby.

www.ingramcontent.com/pod-product-compliance
Lightning Source LLC
LaVergne TN
LVHW041638060526
838200LV00040B/1613